ALTERATIONS

ALTERATIONS

The *Seams Easy* Way

Susan Martinek

Printed in New York by:

OMNIBOOK CO.
99 Wall Street, Suite 118
New York, NY 10005
USA
+1-866-216-9965
www.omnibookcompany.com

First Edition

For e-book purchase: Kindle on Amazon, Barnes and Noble
Book purchase: Amazon.com, Barnes & Noble, and www.omnibookcompany.com

Omnibook titles may be purchased in bulk for educational, business, fund-raising, or sales promotional use. For more information please e-mail **info@ omnibookcompany.com**

Designed by: Gian Carlo Tan

FOREWARD

I began sewing at age ten on a sewing machine. I purchased my own sewing machine while in high school. Sewing was a fun way to create items or add to my wardrobe. Not every item worked out but with failure came lessons on what works and what does not. I worked at two different locations of Younkers retail store (five years each) doing alterations, and then made the decision to open my own business. Seams Easy has been in business for 25 years at this writing. It has been an interesting experience, mostly rewarding, and some frustrating. Doing alterations for this length of time I have been able to devise methods for alterations on different items. I have included some of the basic alterations we did. I was blessed to have some very dedicated employees who tried to do great quality work and provide customer service.

Taking clothing apart for alterations or prepping is very educational. The clothing industry has some applications that work very well. The pattern companies have good directions but do not include some of the better methods, sometimes more complicated methods, for construction. I tried to use machine stitching wherever I could; it is usually quicker, and more secure. As you take clothing items apart, observe the type of application used in the original construction. It may be different from what you are familiar with, and usually there is a good reason why that application was used. My philosophy was to alter items using the quality of original sewing or better, at an affordable price.

Most manufacturers have different size specifications. As a result of that and since our bodies are not always to a standard size, alterations are a real need if a tailored fit is desired. Have you ever been to a professional event and seen a speaker or other professional walk in with their pants dragging or bunched up over their shoes? That does not present a professional image. Hence, job security for those of us doing alterations.

CONTENTS

PART 1

CHAPTER 1
SETTING UP SHOP

ACCOUNTING

We used the QuickBooks program. This worked for us. I would send in the quarterly sales taxes, but I did have an accountant who did all other taxes, and payroll.

CUSTOMER RECEIVING AREA

We used an electronic cash register. We had a 38" x 85" work table that allowed us to use a rotary cutter with mat, and to have the cash register on one end, a computer with monitor unit on the other end, and to be able to still use it to set items on when customers were dropping them off or picking them up. What area you have will dictate how to arrange things you feel necessary.

SEWING EQUIPMENT

Most sewing was done on two Singer 20u33's. A Consew blindstitcher was used for blind hems. A used Viking Husqvarna was purchased as a back-up and for double needle hems. I started out with a newer White serger but then added a good used one for a back-up. Having a good repairman that is able to service your machine in a relatively short amount of time is very helpful. Having a back up machine is a good plan even if it does not do all the functions of your regular one. I was fortunate to purchase a good quality used three way full length mirror from a local store going out of business for a good price.

Clothes Storage and Tracking

I had two racks custom made 98" long and 77" high out of metal pipe that would hold as many heavy items as I put on them. Perhaps you know someone who could make you some? We used one for items "to be altered" and one for items "done". The rack with items "to be done" had rings marked with the days of the week when we promised items would be ready for pickup. We put items to be done behind the ring of the day they were due. It is easy to put an item in the wrong day and we discovered that we all needed to check for items to be in the correct day to catch mistakes. At the beginning of the day we would check at least today's and tomorrow's items to be sure they were all in the correct day, and periodically checked the whole rack. We bought wire hangers when necessary. A few repeat customers would drop off clean used hangers from time to time. Some people recycled hangers from work uniforms being cleaned. We accepted used, clean, "in good shape" hangers. It helped because they are expensive to buy and have to be shipped. We also had a couple wooden racks purchased at a store close out sale that just fit under the pipe racks 8" tall, 23" x 48" we used to hold items that would not hang well. It was neater than placing them on the floor.

If "done items" were left on the rack beyond a reasonable time frame, we would call the customer, to remind them to pick them up. We would document the date, if contact was made, response, and initials of caller on the invoice. We did have a poster on the door stating "Not responsible for garments not picked up within 30 days". We rarely had to liquidate items not picked up, but did a few times, and only after attempts were made to contact the customer numerous times.

Prices

A price list is a good reference tool. New customers really like to take them. It is a way to give customers a price without having to memorize prices. Since all alterable items cannot be included, it gives an idea what general prices are. Determining what to charge is a variable that can be determined by how much time the alteration will require, the degree of difficulty, what notions or fabric will be needed, and what machines are used. You may want to come up with a desired hourly rate that will include your time, and office expenses (broken down into 1 hour). Once that is determined you will be able to arrive at prices per item. Some same type items will go faster than others. An average time should be used to obtain the price. If your prices are too high for your area market, your customers will probably let you know either verbally, or by not having work done. If you have more business than you can do perhaps a rate increase is in order. Experience will help you determine what is right for you. Discuss all prices with all customers, giving an estimate or the actual total for the work to be done when items to be repaired/altered are dropped off. This was one thing that we found invaluable in keeping customers satisfied with our prices. We found that if we discussed the alteration price with our customer before they left the item off, it gave them the power at that time, to decline our work because they were not comfortable with the price. We tried to give estimates on all items dropped off for work to be done. Most customers really appreciated this.

Clean Items

We also had a poster up, "We reserve the right to work on clean garments only". I think some customers just didn't think about items being clean when considering dropping them off for the repairs. This happened mostly with winter coats. If the item was soiled, we would ask them to wash or dry clean the item before we altered it. Most people were okay with it even though it involved another trip. Sometimes we would write the item up and put it in queue to be altered by an agreed upon date. When the customer dropped it off clean, we would match it up with the dated work order.

Office Space

Our office space included three rooms. The largest room was the room customers entered first and our main work room. The middle sized room was used as a Serger/Break Room and housed our two Sergers that did not fit in our first room. One Serger was threaded with black thread since that was the most popular color we used, the other one was used on all other items and we changed thread color as needed. This room also included a cabinet file, a table and chairs, a small refrigerator, and a microwave. It is good to have a place to relax away from the workroom, and to keep food items and crumbs contained. The third, smallest room was used as the fitting room, with three hooks on one wall to hang items, and a bench for customers use as needed.

Payment

Accepting charge cards and debit cards for payments is a service that customers like. There are fees incurred as a result of this, it is not a bad idea to check rates with various service providers before signing a contract. Although there are fees when a transaction goes through you know you have been paid, versus you always have a chance to have a check be returned from the bank. Using a credit card or debit card is the preferred way to pay with our customers. Offering this service also requires more bookwork because of the need to reconcile transactions with the providers' statement and your bank statement. You may want to allow for these expenses when determining your price list.

Accepting checks for payment works well until you have a check returned from the bank for insufficient funds. What we did to get payment then was: call the customer up to three times giving them one week to pay with another type of payment, if this did not happen, we would send them a letter explaining the situation. If no response was given, the next step was to go to the Sheriff's office with a bunch of cash. They did not accept checks. They will serve papers for a fee and mileage for non sufficient funds checks written. This can be added to the original check amount and the bank charges from your bank and submitted in your call/letter for payment from your customer. It is a lot of work to collect this but it may be worth it depending on the amount of the original check. Check with your local Sheriff's office and the process they use.

Pressing Tips

To get the iron at a temperature for almost all fabrics may require some experimentation. It is best to start low and if the temperature does not press wrinkles out it may need to be higher. Use extreme care when pressing delicate fabrics such as silk, or satin. Overpressing may ruin them. Polyester fabrics can melt under too much heat or a shiny fabric may be a result of too much heat. Using a cotton press cloth is a good idea on these types of fabrics.

A pounding block, tailors block, dressmaker ham or sleeve roll can all be used to lay a seam flat during pressing. Steam seam flat and quickly place pounding block or other item over seam with seam laying flat (or fabric where crease is desired) to trap the steam in the seam. Hold for 5 seconds. If flat seam (or crease) is not as crisp as desired repeat this process.

Steam can be an effective tool when a fabric or elastic has been stretched during stitching to shrink it back down. In this situation, let the steam do the work, hold the iron just above fabric or elastic to let the steam penetrate the item. If more shrinking is desired, repeat. In some cases wetting the item (on water safe items only) and allowing it to air dry may help to shrink the stretched out area.

Use equal parts of vinegar and water mixed in a spray bottle to remove old press lines in fabrics that are water safe.

FITTING TIPS

Successful business people know the customer is always right. Making sure the customer looks at, and reviews the fitted/pinned garment is key to keeping redo's to a minimum. Most customers are easy to please the first time keeping this in mind. There are some customers though that have a hard time making up their mind, or are not sure what is best. We had a policy to ask questions until we had a clear image what the customer desired and then fit their garment to that. If the customer was not completely happy we would refit it at the initial fitting. Changing pins is lots easier than realtering a garment. We did not give advice unless the customer requested it. Then we would give some general suggestions and let the customer take it from there. If the customer still could not make up their mind we would give them some time to look in the mirror, to check out the garment while sitting, or whatever helps them come to a decision. If a repeat customer takes a lot of time coming to a decision you may want to charge them a fitting fee in the future. Special undergarments such as a strapless bra or one with a similar fit and shoes or those with the same height heel that will be worn with garment should be worn when fitting the garment. If different height heels will be worn, both shoes should be checked with length pinned. When the garment to be altered is on, have the customer stand in a straight up, looking forward position. Pants should be placed with side seams on sides, and center front and back in place. Pant legs should be hanging straight down. If they bunch up on the shoe or floor they will need to be folded under to achieve a correct length. It is more accurate to mark desired length in the center back of the pants (with no shoe stopping pants from hanging straight). After the back is pinned, front and sides can be pinned for a better visual. Folding under for shortening visually allows you to see the correct length easier. To lengthen, with pants hanging straight down measure in the back from bottom of pant leg to desired length. Always have the customer check the pinned garment. The fitting is the ideal time to adjust.

We used a horizontal finish line pin to mark the length on slacks, skirts, etc. At the fitting, fold up to the finished shorter length desired by the customer and pin. When the garment is being shortened, put a horizontal pin at the bottom of the pinned, folded edge of garment, this will be the desired finish line, where the length of the garment should be when done. When marking how much to lengthen, measure the amount to be lengthened with a ruler from the bottom of garment. Place the horizontal finish line pin that amount above the bottom of garment. Place another pin vertically to make a cross. Crossed pins mean the length needs to be already made longer. The finish line pin should stay in garment until the item is done and being pressed (as an accuracy check) when altering. Interruptions happen and it is a good reminder of where the finish line should be.

When taking a garment in, if the fabric is too thick to pin it together, pins can be placed pointing the angle needed to take the garment in on each side of the seam. A pin placed across can also signify where to start or stop taking in.

When shortening jacket sleeves, fold sleeves up to inside at the desired finished length. It is common to have different length arms. Using a spot on the customers hand to even up different length sleeves or different length arms is the suggested method. For example 1” above the top thumb knuckle, or 1 ½” above the place where the thumb attaches to the hand, etc. Use that same spot on the other hand to make them even. This would be your most accurate pin. After marking front length feel the fabric turned up on the inside. Then try to fold under that same amount around the rest of the sleeve. If a large amount needs to be shortened you may not be able to use this method of folding up the same amount around the sleeve. When fitting for finished length it is better to be more accurate than less accurate. You may really appreciate this when averaging the pinned length.

When altering the sleeve, place a pin at each pinned, folded under area, at the desired finish line. If the jacket sleeves have a mitered seam, and it is trimmed to ¼” or less, it will not be able to be lengthened.

If the item to be altered is a natural fabric (such as raw silk) that has a tendency to shrink, you may want to ask the customer if they have already laundered the item the normal way they will be doing in the future. It will help assure that the item will not shrink up a lot and then be too short or small.

Sewing Tips

When altering, doing all or almost all stitching on the machine was my goal. It usually is stronger, more even, and better looking than hand stitching.

Chalk marks where the cut line is, pins mark where the finish line is, in the hems. Don't mix this if you would like to avoid confusion. Using wax chalk may leave marks when pressed on light colored or light weight fabric. Using clay chalk may leave residue that is hard to remove. The key is to mark so it can be seen while doing the alteration, but not leave a permanent mark. Usually we used wax chalk, but on delicate fabrics white clay chalk or pin marking worked best.

Return all substantial cut off fabric to customer. They may refuse it but if they want it you will be glad to be able to hand it to them.

When cutting off items for shortening, just make a straight across cut, not cutting up the length to cut off and then across. When done you should have a band of fabric. This is a little insurance just in case there is a problem and you need to reattach this fabric because it is too short.

When writing up the work orders it is better to be as specific as you can. If another person is altering the item using your directions, they may not know all you do. I have found name initializing by the person taking in the order is helpful in case there are any questions. Your computer program may be set up for this on the invoice or work order you use.

Always be sure to clip all threads to have a professional looking sew job.

Thread Tension

Check thread tension on every item sewn. Machines will adjust as you go from fabric to fabric. Different threads and different fabrics will need different tensions to be set. See your machine manual for this. A little adjustment may be enough. Most machines will have a tension that works for most things. Remember that amount and go back to that spot after working on an item that required you to change it. This gives you a general correct tension. Thread tension is crucial to good looking and secure stitches.

STITCH LENGTH

When doing alterations check the length of stitches used on the item to be altered or where you are altering. The topstitched stitch length you put in should be the same. To adjust stitch length you can sew over original stitching in the garment, making adjustments to the stitch length if the needle does not go in each stitch at the same spot as original stitching. If you are restitching a seam that will not show it is not as critical. Manufacturers usually have a good reason why they have chosen to use the length of stitch they have used. It may be for strength, perhaps for stretching ability, etc.

THREAD COLOR SELECTION

If you have 500 thread colors, chances are that you will not have the exact color needed some time. If it is in an area where it really shows and you do not have the exact color a close color may be satisfactory. Some of our customers would want exact, others would not require exact, close would be okay. When choosing thread and it is a heavy weight thread, try to duplicate that. Sometimes you can use two same color threads at a time, by threading them through the needle and then topstitching as usual, to make a heavier looking thread. The bobbin will have just one thread as usual. Color supercedes the weight if it is close, unless you are sewing something that requires a heavy duty thread for durability. You cannot always get the exact match, even at the fabric store. Even if you order thread, it may not be the exact color you thought it would be. If you are sewing an item that is flame retardant or flame proof you may need to use a flameproof thread such as Nomex. It is available in a limited color selection. You may not be able to buy this locally but most wholesalers would carry this. When doing new garment construction, select a thread color that is just a shade darker than the fabric. This will blend in when sewn.

Favorite Tools

Having a good tool can really aid in doing a professional job.

Some of my favorite tools include: plastic presser foot lifter, wax and clay chalk, straight edge razor blade, knit picker, spring scissors. SkillTech tempered stainless steel slide ruler in 32nds and mm (I loved these that I found in the hardware store tools department), a spray bottle with an equal parts mixture of white vinegar and water (this helps remove wrinkles, or old pressed in hems, etc. while pressing), skirt marker, long handled ripper, needle threader, curved tip scissors, thread snippers, rotary cutter, pounding block & snag repair tool. Stitching over bumpy seams can break a needle, cause uneven stitches, even make crooked stitches. Using a wedge, Jean-a-ma-jig, Seam buster or even a piece of fabric folded and sewn the same thickness as your seam can eliminate this. All the plastic ones I have used work good, the wedge comes in different heights.

End nippers, and needle nose pliers (shorter nose is stronger) for working on zippers. The nippers can be handy to remove a snap also. Use care not to damage fabric

To attach snaps I used the Press-N-Snap. It is a strong tool that does a good job. Interchangeable dies are needed for different size snaps.

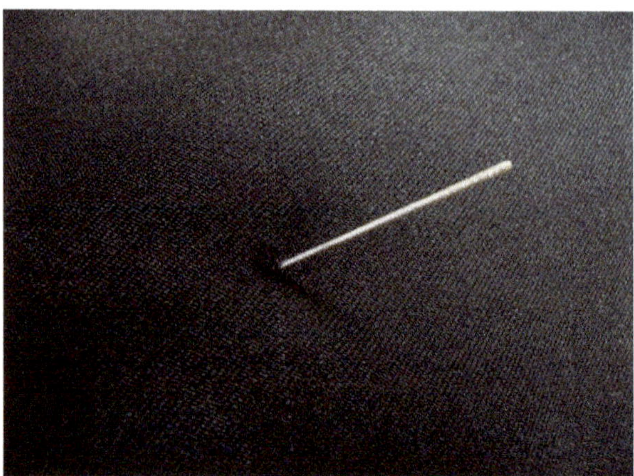

The snag repair tool is a very effective tool, aiding to pull snags to the under side of the garment. After gently stretching garment and steaming it, you will have good results.

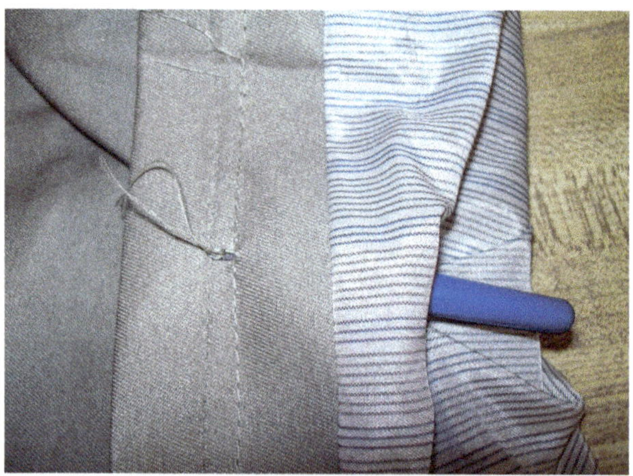

The knit picker will pull threads, even snags to the inside or underside of the garment. It will help to hide threads you may not want to cut.

REMOVING CHAIN STITCHES

Manufacturer machine chain seams can be your friend. Chain straight stitch is a strong stitch. It can easily be removed by finding the right part and pulling it. The tricks are to find the right thread part, and not to open more than you want. A chain stitch can pull out fast, leaving it clean. If only a section of the seam is to be opened, looking at the chain with loops going to the left, I try to break one thread on a loop and then to the right of that cut loop, pull the thread. Once it is clear from the loop, pull on it, it should unravel. Or, cut a loop (if possible) or the chain stitch with the ripper, where you want to start opening the seam, and cut the loop (if possible) or the chain stitch at the location you want to stop removing the stitches. Work threads inside your cut threads only (so you don't unravel any more than you desire).

Work the loops. Practice will improve your success. If the item is not new the original thread may have lint in it, or the thread may be weak, that will make it difficult to unravel. If the manufacturer used wooly nylon thread it may break before you get much pulled.

The loop in the illustration is ready to pull. Once the chain begins to pull, pull right side of the garment threads with one hand and wrong side of the garment thread with the other hand. Tug back and forth with threads. The chain will only pull in one direction. The chain will pull in the opposite direction of the loops. This can only be learned by practicing. Be sure where you stop opening the seam the chain has a tail (not a loop) that will not pull. If the entire seam is to be removed, start at where the stitching stopped originally. Look for thread tails. Garments with a chain stitch can really speed up the prep time for a garment being altered.

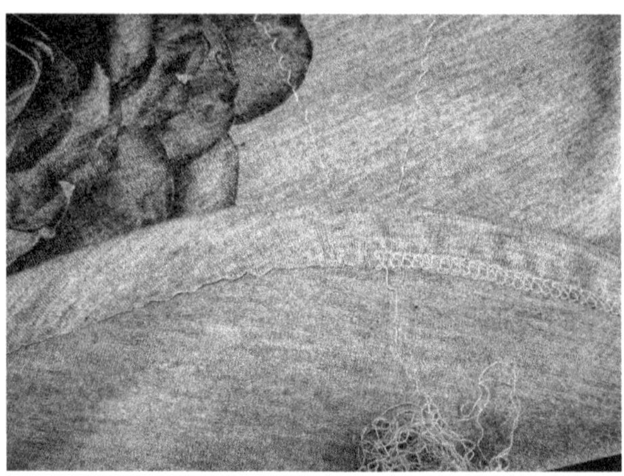

Flat lock stitch is a stitch that is challenging to pull. If the thread is old it can not pull. It will break. It can have lint imbedded and will not pull steadily. It might catch in a textured fabric and not pull. If the thread is a woolly nylon type, it may not pull. It will probably break. But if you do get it to pull, it is great. It is fast and clean.

There are different types of flat lock stitches. There may be 3-5 threads. If you are not removing all stitching be sure to cut the loops on the inside of garment at the start and stop locations before you begin. The chain will pull from the inside (of the garment) loops. If the whole seam is to be pulled out, start at where the stitching was originally stopped. If you cannot find a loop that will pull, go to the outside of the garment and take out the straight stitching. Then try the loops to see if they will pull. The chain will only pull in one direction. This can be best understood by practicing it. Once the chain begins to pull, pull right side of the garment threads with one hand and wrong side of the garment thread with the other hand. Tug back and forth with threads.

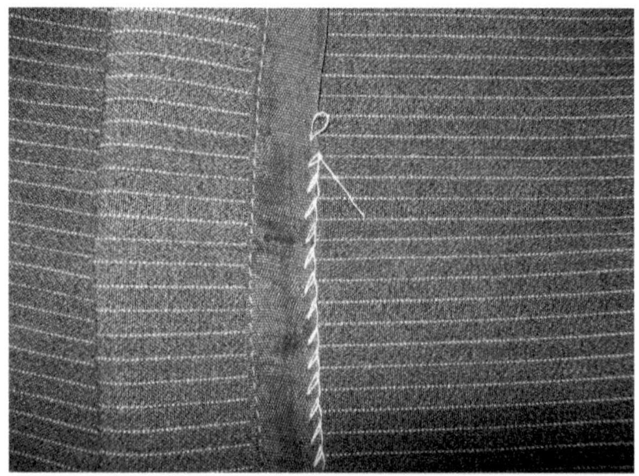

Blind stitch is the stitch used on many hems. The loop in the illustration is ready to pull. Once you get them to pull out, they are fast, and clean since there is only 1 thread. To rip out stitching in a desired location, but not the entire hem, cut the thread of the blindstitching on both ends of area to be removed. Looking at this illustration, release the thread until you have a loop like this. The straight thread is ready and it will pull the stitches out nicely. To lock the blindstitching you must leave a tail that will not pull (try clipping the loop per illustration). Practice will improve your success.

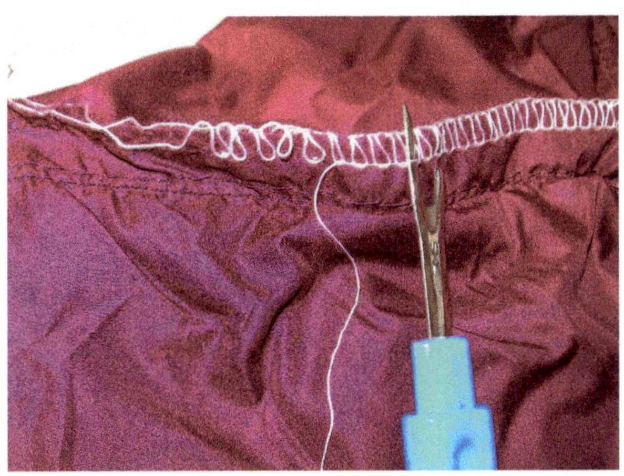

Serged stitch is a neat way to finish off a seam. Since the serger cuts the edge of fabric as it stitches, there is no frayed edge in the stitching. There is a serger ripper with a curved blade on the end, I personally prefer the following methods:

To remove the 3 thread serger stitch, place the ripper under the straight stitching and remove it. This thread can be pulled to gather the fabric until it breaks, then begin again. The other 2 rows will be loose.

To remove the 4 thread serger stitch, place the ripper under the two rows of straight stitching and remove them. Remove one row at a time, or two at a time if possible. The other 2 rows will be loose.

Machine straight stitched seams can be ripped out easier if you pull the thread that has a tighter tension. A lot of times this is the case. Visually you may see which one has a straighter thread line vs. a more rounded (higher) thread line; the straighter one would be the tighter tension thread. Or you can pull the thread on the top and then pull the thread on the bottom until they break, you will see which one is easier. Work from that side, pulling threads until they break.

Since I have enjoyed sewing for so many years, I was happy to find out that my grandma Lillian Hosek (married name Trubl) went to and graduated from Terry Dressmaking School in 1917. She attended this while single. Unfortunately, I didn't discover this until after her death, so I never talked about it with her. It's great to know that we both had an interest in sewing on a more intense level. After marriage she farmed with her husband. Some of the items she made were aprons, clothes pin bags, sun bonnet hats, and her own clothing including denim dresses she wore while "out in the field". I don't know what she originally sewed with, but, eventually she had a The Free treadle sewing machine in an beautiful oak case. It is the machine pictured on the cover of this book.

This dress form was my Grandma's. The apron was hers also.

My Mother also sewed. She started young and made a fabric covered book with sample stitches or techniques she had mastered. This is it.

PART 2
DOING THE ALTERATIONS

CHAPTER 2
SLACKS AND PANTS

If pants need to be shortened, fold them under with the bottom edge at the correct length. Pin hem up to that length using 4 pins distributed around pant leg or more to hold hem up so a good visual can be seen. Most pants are altered straight across. I have found that the center back length is the most accurate one since no shoe is in the way of it laying flat. Sometimes customers request pants to be shorter in front than in the back, this is usually to have less fabric break in the front as it hits the top of the shoe. I have found that a ½" slant works well in most slacks to accommodate this. From time to time customers will request more of a break, or a no break look on the front of the pant leg. Sometimes it works fine, other times it results in a hem that does not lay flat. Letting out the side seams in the hem may alleviate some of this. Another solution may be to put a slit on the outseam at the hem area. If desired see slit directions. Pressing is crucial after alterations. Using a pressing block can make the difference to having a crisp folded edge or not. Pressing block instructions are on page 4.

If pants need to be lengthened, and if there is ample fabric in the hem, measure the amount from the original bottom of the hem to the length the customer desires. Place a pin horizontally that measurement above the original bottom of the hem. Then place a pin vertically at the same spot to form a cross. This means pants are to be lengthened, not shortened. If able, you can place a finish line pin below the existing finish line and omit the crossed pins. Since shortening is more common, this could eliminate a mistake. Perhaps you could put the cross pins in at the fitting and when the customer has taken the garment off you can measure the amount to be lengthened and move it to the amount below the existing finish line on the inside of pant leg in the hem. The finish line pin should stay in the garment until the item is done, and being pressed, as an accuracy check when altering. Interruptions happen and it is a good reminder of where the finish line should be.

Fittings can be interesting. Susan Blad, a former employee, recalls the following 2 fittings she did: I pinned a gentleman's dress slacks for waist and seat in, he came out of the fitting room holding his pants up and said "We have a problem here." I had pinned his underwear too! Another time, I, being 5' tall did a fitting for a woman who is 6' 2". I had to get on the step stool to pin the shoulders of her tank top. Her little girl snickered through the entire fitting.

MEN'S PLAIN BOTTOM SLACKS

1. Put a pin at the desired finish line at each place pants are pinned under, if length is to be averaged. Average pins. Place one pin that amount at the desired finish line. Remove other pins. If center back pin is the most accurate one and pants are to be shortened straight across put a pin at the folded edge of the pinned up hem at center back. This is your finish line pin.

2. Cut off 2 ¼" longer than finish line or amount of original hem. If leg is tapered, hem should be small enough to lay smooth. Most dress pants are cut straight enough at the bottom of the leg to be able to do this. If not enough fabric is available for this size hem, make as the hem the manufacturer has done or as wide as you can. If pants are tapered this may not work, the seams could be let out through the underside hem, if desired, so a wider hem may be used. To do this, start at the desired finish line length and let out through the hem, in the side seams matching hem width to pant leg above the desired finish line.

3. Serge cut edge of slacks turning seams towards back of slacks, or as original.

4. Pin up 2 ¼" hem for men's slacks, lining up side seams and center front and center back crease lines so hem lays flat. Blindstitch at inside of serging (about ¼" from serged edge). *Do an accuracy check to be sure all stitches catch and that they are not too deep. I found that if you adjust the stitch to where it is catching on most stitches and then adjust just a little until they are all caught you are in the right depth. After stitching a quarter of way around hem, check blindstitching depth, if okay, continue to end. Overlap stitching an inch or two. When cutting thread, be sure to cut in the loop so it will not pull out if pulled on. Check stitch depth on entire next leg to be sure it remain constant. A good quality hem may need to be done more than once, to make sure stitch depth is the correct adjustment.*

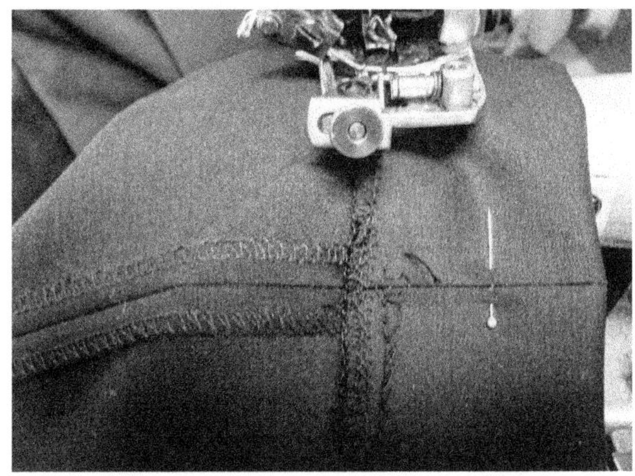

5. Press from inside first and then from top only using enough pressure to lay hem flat.

WOMEN'S PLAIN BOTTOM SLACKS

1. Put a pin at the desired finish line at each place pants are pinned under if length is to be averaged. If the center back pin is the most accurate one, and the pants are to be shortened straight across, put a pin at the folded edge of the pinned up hem. This is your finish line pin.

2. Cut off 1 ½" longer than finish line or amount of original hem (if leg is tapered, hem should be small enough to lay smooth).

3. Serge edge of slacks turning seams towards slacks back or as original.

4. Pin up 1 ½" hem, or amount of original hem, lining up side seams and center front and center back crease lines so hem lays flat. Blindstitch at edge of serging, catching edge of hem. Do an accuracy check to be sure all stitches catch and that they are not too deep. I found that if you adjust the stitch to where it is catching on most stitches and then adjust just a little until they are all caught you are in the right depth. You may need to press the hem to be sure how hem will look after pressing. After stitching a quarter of way around hem check blindstitching depth, if okay, continue to end. Overlap stitching an inch or two. When cutting thread, be sure to cut in the loop so it will not pull out if pulled on. Check stitch depth on entire next leg to be sure it remains constant. A good quality hem may need to be done more than once, to make sure stitch depth is the correct adjustment.

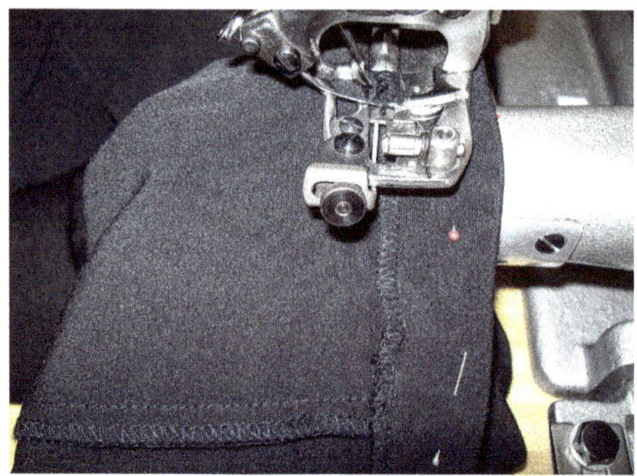

5. Press from inside first and then from top only using enough pressure to lay hem flat.

WOMEN'S SLACKS WITH HEM TAPE

If hem tape was used on the original hem, it needs to be removed and reused, if in good condition. I tried to alter items to original quality or better. If pant leg gets wider and pants are shortened a bunch you may need to add more hem tape to go around the complete pant leg. If you try to make it fit you may end up with a gathered looking hem. Have hem tape sewn on with plenty of give. Duplicating original hem width would be advised.

PANTS WITH A SLIT

Usually a slit is placed on the outseam of pants. First determine amount of slit. Mark area of slit to stop above bottom of pants with a pin. Open up outseam to that pin above finish line. Stitch over existing seam stitching above slit pin and backstitch to reinforce seam. Mark hem line with a pin on each side exactly opposite each other.

Fold pants at hem with right sides together with pin being at the bottom edge. Do not stitch over pin, remove it just before getting to it. Stitch in seam, backstitching at hemline, making sure hem is laying flat, with finish line on bottom edge up just to the end of the slit, backstitch. Turn right side out. Pant should lay flat with hem at bottom edge. On other side of slit, stitch in seam backstitching at hemline, making sure hem is laying flat with finish line on bottom edge, up to the end of the slit, backstitch to top edge of hem.

Turn right side out. Pant should lay flat with hem at bottom edge. Trim seams if needed. Duplicate original finish of hem and top stitch if original was. Do other leg as first was done. Press.

Lined Slacks

Shorten outside layer to length pinned with a blindstitched hem or as original hem. Most linings are not sewn to outside layer of pants at hem as per these instructions. Some are though and it works quite well. Safety pin crotch of lining to crotch of slacks at thigh/crotch cross seam. Hold slacks at waist with one hand and following outseam of slacks and outseam of lining go to hem. Now, holding both slacks and lining on outseam at hem, tug gently so fabrics relax in alignment under your grip. Pin lining to slacks near hem at this alignment. Go to inseam, grip lining and slacks at hem, gently tug so fabrics are relaxed in alignment under your grip. Pin lining to slacks near hem at this alignment. Take center of lining at hem and center of slacks at hem and tug gently with one hand on waistband and with other hand grip hem until a relaxed alignment is achieved on both center front and center back. Any excess lining width should be distributed evenly between all four pins at hem line. (If slacks are wide, more pins securing the lining to the slacks may be necessary.) This is to assure the lining will be the correct length. Cut lining to be ½" longer than finished slacks. Leave one pin in a seam to hold lining to slacks if connectors have been used and will need to be reattached, pin may need to be moved up seam to be out of the way. Press lining under ½". Turn that under 1" and straight stitch hem.

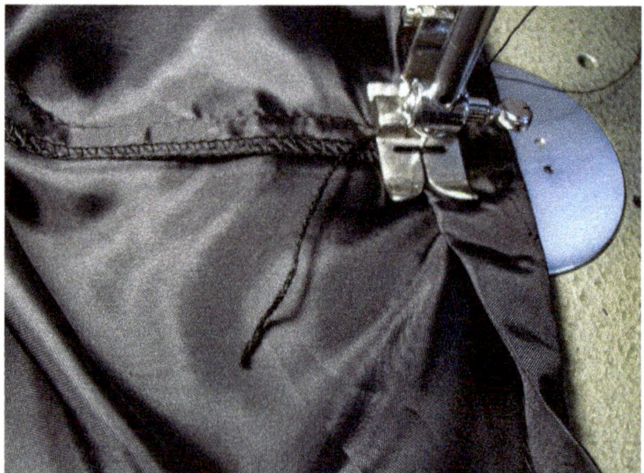

Finished lining length should be 1" shorter than slacks. Connectors can be used to keep lining in place.

If the manufacturer has used them, we put them back in if they are usable, if not, we make some by serging a length of thread about 2" long at the seams near the hem to hold outseam and/or inseam lining in position next to slack.

Remove safety pin in crotch and any others. Press.

WOMEN'S LINED SLACKS ATTACHED AT THE HEM

Follow instructions for lined slacks through the slack cutting instructions. Cut the same amount off of the lining as the outside layer. Leave one pin attaching lining to slacks near hem on each leg. Pin slacks up to correct hem length in center front and back. Turn slacks inside out. To hold hem exactly in place at the side seams, place a pin across the seam at the place to fold up the hem (matching hem amount pinned in front and back). At the side seam bottom, fold the slack side seam and the hem side seam together, at finish line pin. In seam, stitch the hem and slacks side seams together from the fold to about 5/8" from cut edge of hem. On first leg: From the pin holding leg seams together, with right sides together, line up the lining and slacks cut edges to same seams as pinned. Pin slacks and lining together with side seams lined up, as well as the center front and center back. Using a ½" seam, sew around entire pant leg. The lining may have a bit of excess fabric; if so ease it in as you sew. Stitching with the lining down and the slack fabric up is a good way to let the feed dog of your machine help you ease it in. Overlap stitching 1". Remove finish line pin at side seams. Remove pin holding lining to slacks.

On the second leg: repeat hem stitching as on leg one except only attach lining to slacks around ¾ of pant leg. Remove finish line pin at side seams. Remove pin holding lining to slacks. Turn slacks right side out through this opening. Slacks will need to be blindstitched to hold hem in place. Pin hem evenly by measuring hem from lining seam to hem minus ½" (the amount in the seam).

Stitch line should be just below where lining attaches to slacks hem. Stitch first leg, then stitch second leg, blindstitching the lining opening shut. Press with steam, being cautious not to over press.

LENGTHENING A GARMENT THAT IS NOT NEW

If the old stitch line shows, you will need to use that for your straight line when cutting off and putting the hem back in. Using vinegar and water sprayed over the old fold line helps to lessen the old line. After spraying, use a press cloth and iron over the old fold line until the liquid evaporates. Repeat if desired. If old stitch holes are left in the garment, they can be brushed with a clean toothbrush to close them somewhat. If the garment is being lengthened, stitching over the old fold line helps to hide it.

A facing can be added and the hem can be pinned up, and then stitched from the outside over the old fold line. Or it can be pinned up and restitched over the original stitch line. Where the edge of the hem is will help to determine what method to use.

Another way is to stitch over the old fold line, and then blind stitch the hem in place. It is a good way to deceive the eye about the lengthening process.

Certainly, a blindstitch hem can be used with the hem let down and repositioned alone (without a topstitching line) also.

Lengthening Slacks or Other Items with Hem Tape

I usually used the cotton wide single fold bias tape, it has ¼" folded under on each side. If the fabric is light weight or light in color, you may need to go to a finer tape such as a polyester hem or seam tape. Line up the hem tape with about ⅜" excess length beyond the slack inseam (this is to seam together the facing when it has been attached). The hem tape and slacks cut edge should be even with edges placed one over the other. Place presser foot about ⅜" in front of the inseam. Backstitch to the inseam in a ¼" seam. At inseam, stitch forward and around the entire slack leg and back to the inseam.

Backstitch. The beginning and end of this seam should be to the inseam, not over. Turn facing so right sides are together at inseam. Stitch a seam so facing is the same width as the slack leg.

Trim seam to ¼". Press seam open. Press facing away from slacks, using caution not to press out the ¼" pressed under edge of the bias tape on the unsewn side. Pin up to desired length. On outside of slacks, check to be sure all seams are straight near hem when pinning up (the facing may pull a seam one way or another).

Hem. Press with steam, being cautious not to over press.

Double Needle Hem

1. Cut garment to be ⅛" plus the original hem length longer than finish line pin (if original hem is 1" cut ¹ ⅛" longer than finish line pin).

2. Serge cut edge turning seams towards back of garment or as original.

3. Pin hem up with pins being close to folded edge about 2" apart.

4. Place a piece of tape or other guide on the right side of the presser foot directly on the sewing machine bed ⅛" shorter than hem (if hem is 1 ⅛", line guide up to be 1" from center of double needles). *This will help keep your stitching straight, and aligns you sewing directly over the edge of your hem.* Lay garment right side up with hem edge just at the seam guide. Make sure both layers are laying flat.

5. Begin stitching (at the inseam for slacks, in the back or side seam for a skirt or dress), hold the hem straight butting the edge along the seam guide as you go. *If the fabric is a stretchy or knit fabric, slightly stretching it while stitching should allow the thread tension to be loose enough to be stretched without the thread breaking while being worn. Be sure to stretch it and check the tension when alterations are completed. If the thread is stopping the fabric from stretching, you will need to adjust the thread tension or the stretch amount during stitching and redo. To stitch this straight requires some practice. Keeping/holding the same stretch while stitching is key, letting the machine feed the fabric through.* Overlap stitching about an inch. Check to make sure hem is caught by the stitching. If the hem is caught almost entirely, is laying flat, you can handstitch it to the bobbin thread from the underside (so no extra stitches show from the outside). The double needle hem really shows, it looks much better if the entire hem is done in one pass. Also check for skipped stitches, if you have some they can be caught by handstitching them from the underside.

6. Press. If the fabric was stretched while stitching it may have a wavy seam. Use steam to help it to flatten out as you press.

WarmUp Pants with Zippers at the Hem

This method shortens the zippers as the pants are shortened. Usually this is okay with the customer. **Be sure to ask the customer if it's okay. To remove and resew zipper as original is time consuming and the alteration price needs to reflect that.**

WarmUp Pants with Elastic at Hem

To fit for the correct length on lower pant leg: pinch fabric together horizontally about 4" above bottom of pant leg the amount that needs to be shortened, and safety pin. Continue doing this around entire pant leg. Be sure to state in alteration directions that this is the amount to be shortened, not that this is the new bottom of the pants. And/or pin a note to the pants at hem stating "Shorten pants by removing amount pinned". Open original hem and remove elastic. Take note of construction method. Detach zipper in seam at hem and up to just above the desired finish line. Average amount from pin to fold of fabric. The measured amount will need to be doubled. (The fabric in the pin is doubled, hence the total amount to be shortened is doubled.) For lined pants: unzip zippers, smooth lining out to be flat from hem up, safety pin (about 6-8" above hem) a line holding lining in place across entire pant leg.

1. Place a desired finish line pin at both sides of fabric at zipper opening. Place pins along the finish line about 3" apart. *These will be the fold line for the hem.* With zipper open, cut zipper to be ½"-1" beyond than the finish line.

2. Cut pants fabric off amount to be shortened. If pants are lined, cut lining off the same amount. Lining needs to be basted to pants so it will be the correct length when completed. Baste lining to pants with a ¼" seam starting/stopping about 1-2" from each open end. *This method will work if pants were constructed with this method (usual way) or if pants are to be shortened more than 2". If lining is too short, follow original placement method used by manufacturer.*

3. Attach elastic to hem at zipper as original. With pants turned under at finish line pin, round zipper to inside of pant hem. Top stitch pant to zipper (if originally top stitched), if not, sew as original. Repeat as for other side. When zipper is zipped, the bottom needs to be even. If lined, lining may need to be sewn to zipper, or it may tuck inside of hem.

4. If the cut edge of the hem will be folded under, press that amount towards inside along the bottom edge. If lined, lay with lining flat and to bottom of hem fold at finish line pins, pin hem. Start at inseam, align seams to be one on top of the other. Pin the rest of the hem, evenly distributing fabric. If pants are tapered, and the hem is too narrow to lay flat, the inseam will need to be let out in the hem. Elastic will need to be stretched as sewing, if elastic is stitched in hem it will need to be evenly distributed. Start at top of hem by zipper, (with hem edge even with outside fabric on zipper) stitch hem along edge to finish line pin.

Turn and sew back up to top of hem. Turn pants hem right side out and stitch along top of hem with the hem depth the same as original.

At end of hem turn and stitch down to finish line pin, turn and stitch up edge of hem. Cut threads.

5. Top stitch second row of stitching if there was another one originally. Top stitch at zipper if there was any other stitching originally. Press, using caution not to put the iron directly on top of the zipper.

Warm Up Pants with Zipper and Plain Bottom

Fit pants by folding extra length under and pin to desired length. Average amount pinned up. Place a finish line pin the averaged amount up from bottom of pant. Follow elastic at hem method, ignoring the elastic directions.

Cuffed Hems

Cuffed hems directions are for light weight fabrics such as twill, cotton, gabardine. When using heavy weight fabric such as corduroy wool, etc. add ¼" to amount in the hem.

1" Cuffed Pant Hem

1. Cut pant to be 3" longer than finish line pin.

2. Serge edge laying seams towards pant back or as original.

3. Pin and blindstitch a 2" hem.

4. Fold the hem up into a scant 1" cuff. Stitch in the ditch (sew directly over the side seams of cuff, so stitching shows only slightly) side seams 1" cuff beginning at bottom, up the cuff, turn at top of cuff, stich back down cuff to bottom.

5. Press (and use pounding block) cuff, measuring center front and back cuff to be even with side seam cuff.

1 ¼" Cuffed Pant Hem

1. Cut pant to be 3 ¾" longer than finish line pin.

2. Serge edge laying seams towards pant back or as original.

3. Pin and blindstitch a 2 ½" hem.

4. Fold the hem up into a scant 1 ¼" cuff. Stitch in the ditch (sew directly over the side seams of cuff, so stitching shows only slightly) side seams 1 ¼" cuff beginning at bottom, up the cuff, turn at top of cuff, stich back down cuff to bottom.

5. Press (and use pounding block) cuff, measuring center front and back cuff to be even with side seam cuff.

1 ½" Cuffed Pant Hem

1. Cut pant to be 4 ½" longer than finish line pin.

2. Serge edge laying seams towards pant back or as original.

3. Pin and blindstitch a 3" hem.

4. Fold the hem up into a scant 1 ½" cuff. Stitch in the ditch (sew directly over the side seams of cuff, so stitching shows only slightly) side seams 1 ½" cuff beginning at bottom, up the cuff, turn at top of cuff, stich back down cuff to bottom.

5. Press (and use pounding block) cuff, measuring center front and back cuff to be even with side seam cuff.

2" and Wider Cuffed Pants

Hem should be put back as manufacturer has constructed. Below are guidelines on one type of wide cuff. Doing only one leg at a time allows you to have one to go back to throughout the alteration process if you have any questions.

1. Measure the amount to be shortened or lengthened, average if necessary. Record amount on paper for possible future reference. Measure width of cuff. Record on paper.

2. Measure amount in hem after cuff is let down. Record on paper.

3. Place a pin, (safety pins stay put) the amount to be shortened above each of the three old fold lines (top of cuff, and bottom of cuff outside fabric and inside fabric). If pants are to be lengthened, place pins at amt. to be lengthened below three old fold lines. Press old fold lines out. Use a 50% vinegar and 50% water mix in a spray bottle and a pounding block for best results.

4. *Cut off amount to be shortened. If pants are to be lengthened, fabric availability in hem will determine the maximum amount they can be lengthened.*

5. *The middle pin marks where hem fold line should be. Sew hem as original.*

6. *Fold up cuff to original width. Make sure sides and centers are the same width, sometimes the stitched area at side seam will stretch when sewn. Stitch side seams starting at bottom, turning at top of cuff and stitching back down to bottom. Blindstitch in place ½"-¾" below top of cuff adjusting blindstitcher so inside layer of cuff catches but not outside layer. You may have to stitch only on area with no side seams to have a consistent stitch. If so, start and stop just beyond side seams, hand stitch remaining hem not blindstitched.*

7. *Press using pounding block, measuring center front and back cuff to be even with side seam cuff.*

Reattaching Fabric for a Cuff

Instructions are for thin fabric such as twill, cotton. For a heavy fabric add ¼" to fabric amount being reattached using the rest same measurements.

This method is for when fabric has been cutoff and needs to be reattached for a cuff, or if you have more same fabric to be used to add a cuff.

Mark where finished length is to be with a pin on pant leg. Determine width of cuff with customer. I will use a 1 ½" cuff for this example. Cut pants to be 1 ½" longer than finish line pin if fabric is longer than that. If less than this fabric is available do not cut any off. The amount that the bottom of pant leg is short of finish line will need to be added to the amount to reattach. For example if pant leg is ½″ shorter than the desired finish line of cuff, an additional ½″ will need to be added to the amount to reattach. The reattach seam will need to be covered in the cuff so you have a limit to amount you can be short of finish line. In a ¼″ seam reattach fabric to pant leg matching side seams closely. Press seam open using a pounding block or a piece of wood after steaming. See pounding block instructions on page 4.

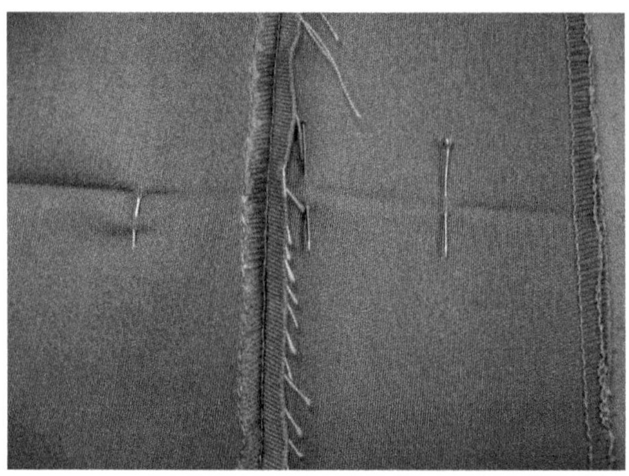

Place a pin 1 ½″ (or amount of cuff) below finish line pin in hem, this will be the top edge of finished cuff. Place another pin 1 ½″ (or amount of cuff) below that, this will be the bottom edge of finished cuff. Cut line ideally will be chalked 1 ½″ (or amount of cuff) or at least ½″ below the second pin, this will be the hem on the inside of pant cuff. If you have allowed 1 ½″ for the last measurement pin, you will have a 3″ (or double the width of cuff) hem in pants. If you have a small amount of fabric for the last measurement/hem on the inside of pant leg, you can use less, but it must be at least 3/8″. Use the original measurements only changing the last one. To accurately secure that amount in place, make a line of pins (about 2″ apart) through both thicknesses, near the cut edge of pants to hold the hem in place. Stitch hem using a blindstitch for dress slacks and straight stitch for casual pants. Do not press yet. Fold cuff up, measuring on the top of cuff to be 1 ½″ (or amount of cuff), stitch in the ditch from the bottom to the top, turning and stitching to bottom of cuff first. Cut threads. Press cuff by folding cuff in center to be exact width of cuff at side seams. Use a pounding block to make a crisp cuff, re-creasing front and back centers if done so originally. To keep cuff in place, especially good for wide hems, blind stitch in place ½″-¾″ below top of cuff adjusting blindstitcher so inside layer of cuff catches but not outside layer. You may have to stitch only on area with no side seams to have a consistent stitch. If so, start and stop just beyond side seams.

WOMEN'S SLACKS WAIST AND SEAT TAKEN IN

Directions are for slacks with a zipper in the center front. To fit: have customer face mirror, pinch fabric to be taken in at top of waistband or where needed at center back seam; going down seam, pinch fabric to be taken in, placing additional pins 2-3" apart having pins in the exact location seam needs to be taken in. A horizontal pin marking where to stop can be placed in seam. If seat needs to be taken in lower than you can place a pin you will need to round/ taper seam from last placed pin through crotch curve. Do not take in crotch seam beyond curve at end where inseam meets crotch seam. After fitting, garment fabric should lay evenly in back when on, not pulling in any direction. *Keep in mind if you take too much in at center back waist, the waistband may scoop down some in center back when garment is on.* If there is a large amount to be taken in you may need to take in both side seams instead of just the center back seam or in addition to it. If the crotch hangs low it may need to be taken in also. If so, you may want to start giving prices to the customer so they know what doing multiple alterations will cost. It may or may not be worth it to them to do so. To bring the crotch up, the thigh will need to be taken in.

To fit for crotch up: grasp seat seam fabric together amount to be taken in. Place a pin horizontally holding this fabric. Just below the crotch, in the back of the thigh, grasp the same amount of fabric that is to be taken in through the crotch and place a pin vertically. The amount to be taken in at the top of the inseam will need to match the amount taken in at the crotch (pinned in at the seat). Place additional pins 3"-4" apart down center back of leg with the amount needed to be taken in. You may be able to stop at knee area, at calf area, or you may need to go through hem.

1. Chalk pins on wrong side of garment. If garment is lined you will need to go under that. Lining may be open at hem. If lining is attached at hem, you will need to open waistband and detach lining to get inside to chalk pins. Measure the amount to be taken in at waist, record. Remove pins. Detach waistband including the center back seam through the side that the button is located. Mark with a chalk dot or safety pin where button will be relocated (over the amount waistband is to be taken in). Detach button. Mark new end of waistband with a pin and then chalk on wrong side of fabric. If waistband extended past center front of slacks with a seam in bottom of waistband, record that amount or place safety pin (over the amount waistband is to be taken in) at new location of end of seam at bottom of waistband.

2. On inside of slacks, if chalk lines are not even from the center back seam on both sides of slacks they will need to be averaged from the seam. Stitch center back seam of slacks over averaged chalk lines. Restitch over first stitching. Backstitch. Trim seat seam to original width or just a little wider. Serge seam. If slacks are lined, take lining in the same amount as slacks. Trim and serge seam.

3. Press seam open or as original. Press lining seam flat. Baste lining to slacks ¼" from raw edge across top of slacks where opened.

4. Finish button end of waistband as original to the shorter length. If waistband was extended beyond center front of slacks, duplicate as original.

5. Pin button end of waistband to slacks center front or opening, extend as original amount. Evenly distribute band to slacks and pin in place. *This can be a job that 3 hands work better than two. To get some help, what I would do sometimes, is to place the waistband under the presser foot. Put the presser foot down, then hold slacks/waistband away from machine, thus getting an even distribution. Place a pin in the center holding waistband and slacks together, place a pin in the center of that, repeat until pinned every 2-4".* With the same seam size as original, attach waistband as original, overlapping original stitching at just before center back seam, stitch in fold of waistband with right side to right side of slacks. Stop at slacks center front/button end, backstitch.

6. Back of waistband will need to be attached. Usually the back is attached by stitching in the ditch of the waistband seam catching back of waistband. *This can be tricky to achieve. You may need to hand baste back in place first.* Pin waistband in place making sure all is flat before stitching. Be sure when machine stitching that waistband is feeding evenly into machine.

7. Press. Resew button at chalk dot or safety pin (should be directly at top of zipper).

Women's Slacks Waist and Seat Let Out

Womens slacks may or may not be able to be let out. Places to let out are: side seams, center front or back seams, darts, pleats. **Things to tell the customer: you may have to add a piece of fabric to waistband and it may not match exactly. If the customer is concerned, suggest they go to the fabric store and find a suitable fabric for use. Seams let out in slacks may or may not show, chances they will show increase, as the age of the slacks increases.** Letting out darts or pleats to enlarge waist and seat would be my preferred location to let out. Determine if the customer needs more let out in the front area or the back area (by their body type). That is the area to let out. To fit for letting out waist and seat area: measure slacks on customer with waistband unbuttoned and zipper unzipped. Measure amount from button to ¼" inside buttonhole on side closest to the button. That is the amount to let waistband out. Place a pin that amount parallel from top of zipper or record amount. Go down to middle of zipper, measure amount from zipper side to zipper side. Place a pin that distance from one side of zipper or record amount. Place a horizontal pin at location to stop letting slacks out or record location. If slacks need to be let out below darts, side seams will need to be the location let out. There is no exact way to measure that. Gauge amount needed by the amount needed to let out at and above zipper. This is an alteration that may need multiple attempts to get right.

1. Detach waistband through seam/seams to be let out through button end of waistband.

2. Determine amount to be let out and from where. For example, if 1" needs to be let out through the front of slacks and there are 2 front darts, let each dart out ½" or resew the dart seam ¼" over from the original (there is ¼" on each side of dart, hence a total of ½" per dart). *Some darts are marked with a mark that could be visible if let out all the way. If so, you will need to leave at least a narrow seam with the mark in it. Some darts are marked with a small hole cut into slacks. If so, you will need to leave at least a narrow seam with the cut in it.* If slacks are lined, let them out as the slacks have been. Remove original dart or seam stitching. Press darts to center.

3. The waistband or facing will need to be extended the amount let out in the waist of the slacks. Find a similar color and weight fabric for this. Measure the entire width of the waistband: front, the front seam, the back waistband fabric and seam or turn under. Add a little room for error if desired. This can always be trimmed later. Length of fabric should be the amount to be let out plus ½" (for a ¼" seam where attached and at end). Interface fabric for

waistband as original waistband is. Mark with chalk or a pin on extension where button will go (the amount to be let out over from original placement). Mark with chalk or a pin on extension where end of waistband will be (the amount to be let out over from original end of waistband). Mark with a pin or chalk where extension is seamed at bottom as original.

4. Open up end of waistband. With front edges even, stitch extension onto waistband in a ¼" seam. Backstitch both ends. Press seam open. Trim to exact width needed. Finish waistband back as original, with serging, turned under, hem tape, etc. With right sides of waistband button end together, fold along top edge. Stitch end as original was done at marked location. Trim seam. Turn right side out. *You may want to gently push corners out with a pointed wooden dowel or similar tool.* Waistband should lay flat and even. Press.

5. Pin end of waistband to garment center front or opening, extending as original amount. Evenly distribute band to slacks and pin in place. *This can be a job that 3 hands work better than two. To get some help, what I would do sometimes, is to place the waistband under the presser foot, put the presser foot down, then hold slacks/waistband away from machine, thus getting an even distribution. Place a pin in the center holding waistband and slacks together, place a pin in the center of that, repeat until pinned every 2-4".* With the same seam size as original, attach waistband as original, overlapping original stitching at start, stitch in fold of waistband with right side to right side of garment. Stop at center front/button end, backstitch.

6. Attach the inside of waistband as the manufacturer did originally. Usually the back is attached by stitching in the ditch of the waistband seam catching back of waistband. If the waistband was topstitched at waist seam, do so. *This can be tricky to achieve. You may need to hand baste back in place first.* Pin waistband in place, making sure all is flat before stitching. Be sure when machine stitching that waistband is feeding evenly into machine and not bunching or being pushed or pulled by the presser foot.

7. Press. Resew button at chalk dot or safety pin (should be directly at top of zipper).

Shortening Elastic Waist Pants from the Waist

Elastic waist pants can be shortened from the waist making the crotch and pants shorter. To determine amount to be shortened, safety pin amount of fabric to be shortened below the waistband all the way around. Pants should hang evenly from waist down after pinning. To be sure the customer will have enough room to comfortably sit, have them sit down after pants have been pinned. If the amount is close to the same amount all the way around it can be averaged. If a smaller or larger amount is to be shortened in an area it will need to be marked and shortened that amount in that area. To determine how much, in what area, chalk the top and bottom fabric at inside of pants at each safety pin. When the safety pin is removed the amount to shorten at that spot will be between the chalk lines. Remove the elastic from pants, cut off that amount or the averaged amount to be shortened. If elastic is to be stitched down in waistband, it will need to be evenly distributed. If not already done, sew elastic together to original length into a circle. Mark elastic seamed area as back of elastic with a pin, hold elastic together at the pin, run other hand to the end of the elastic circle, placing a pin there. This is your center front. Pin back elastic to pants center back seam and the other pin to front seam. Stretching pants from center back to center front, pin elastic to side seam. (To aid doing this, put one section under the presser foot, put it down, it will firmly hold waistband, and you gain the use of a hand.) Pin elastic to other side seam also. At this point, elastic is usually serged to pants at the top inside edge of pants. Stitch as original waist. Line up inside waistband seams (at center back, center front, etc.) to be straight with outside ones. If a casing was used as the original application, cut off fabric, stitch casing down as original leaving a 2" opening. Insert elastic leaving ends out. Making sure elastic is not twisted in casing, overlap and sew as original length. Sew casing shut. Adjust elastic by stretching waistband numerous times until elastic is evenly distributed. If topstitching was used, pin in position at seams and topstitch as original. If there is no topstitching stitch in the ditch at side seams or above side seams and center front to keep elastic from rolling when laundered. Steam, lightly pressing.

WOMEN'S ELASTIC WAIST PANTS SIDES IN

Sides can be taken in on the outseam or on the inseam or both. If the pants are too big through the waist and hip area, probably taking them in on the outseam is best. If pants are too low through the crotch they will need to be taken in at the inseam. If they need to be taken in between the hip and hem, they could be taken in on the inseam, or the outseam, or both, if the amount is substantial. If outseam and inseam are both being taken in, ideally they should be taken in an equal amount. If the crotch is taken up through the inseam, taking the inseam in through the thigh and down may be the best option. To take in pant legs from hip down, you probably will need to take ½ of the amount to be taken in on the outseam, and ½ of the amount on the inseam, to be sure the grain and possibly the fabric print of slacks will hang straight. The amount to be taken in may help determine 1 or 2 seams taken in on each leg. Try to create a smooth line on slacks. They should lay flat on outseam and inseam if possible. Some people have different size hips and each side may need to be marked and taken in that amount.

To mark the crotch up, grasp the seat seam and pinch together the amount to be taken up and place a pin horizontally holding that amount. Just below the crotch, in the center back pant leg, grasp amount to be taken in through the leg and place a pin vertically. Place additional pins 3-4" apart down center back of leg with the amount needed to be taken in. You may be able to stop at knee area, at calf area, or you may need to go all the way through the hem. *The amount to be taken in at the top of the inseam will need to match the amount taken in at the crotch (pinned in at the seat).*

Pin the amount to be taken in on outseam beginning at the side where needed, about every 3-4", as needed. Point pins the angle needed to start/stop taper. A pin placed across can signify where to start or stop taking in.

1. Average pins across from each other on inseams and outseams if customer is even.

2. Chalk fabric on each side of pins on inside of pants. Using wax chalk may leave marks when pressed on light colored or light weight fabric. Clay chalk does not usually leave marks, but may, especially the colored chalk on a white item. Remove pins. Open waistband, if needed, to get into seam area at top of side.

Hint: If the pocket edge lays along side seam you may need to take pockets apart and move them over amount to be taken in. This requires a lot more time

3. Sew over original stitched seam 1" before the point to begin, and again where you end, taking in the seam. Stitch along chalk lines making sure seam is relatively straight. If the seam needs to go through hem or waistband, backstitch at end.

4. Remove the original seam stitching, leaving a 1" stitiching overlap where the altered seam begins.

5. Trim seam to original width or just a little wider. Serge edge.

6. Press seam either open or to the back of the pants as the original. If pants had a crease in the center front or center back it may need to be moved. If so, press out old crease from the wrong side of pants first. Use an even combination of vinegar and water in a spray bottle to aid in removing old crease lines as you press.

Hint: Some pants have permanent crease lines and will not be movable. This is something that is good to establish at the fitting if possible to alert the customer to. If pants are new they may have a tag that states they have a permanent crease. Some fabrics will need a press cloth over the fabric. If in doubt, use one. To make a new crease, on the ironing board, lay slacks with the hem even at the bottom and the inseam laying over the outseam. Begin pressing the crease where the tapering ended, using steam. Clap pounding block immediately over the slack edge, to block the steam in. After 5 seconds, remove block and repeat process where new crease stopped. Continue to crotch area. If pants are pleated in front at the waist, the crease will need to go to the pleat. Give preference to front crease looking straight when lining up with pleat and front crease. The inseam laying directly over the outseam at the crotch area, may need to be tweaked just a bit, to be straight, if slacks were taken in a lot. See how they look when you hold them at the waistband and the crease falls as it is. If there is no pleat, stop crease at crotch.

Docker Type Hem

1. Cut pant to be 1⅝" longer than finish line pin.

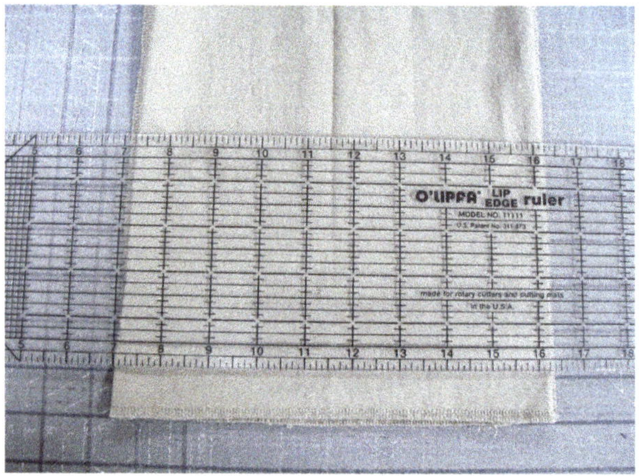

2. Press under ½".

3. Hem with 1⅛" top stitched hem using a wedge under the back of the presser foot when stitching over the seams (so the presser foot is level).

MEN'S TROUSER WAIST IN

1. Mark the amount to be taken in at the back of pants waistband and through the seat as needed. Sometimes the seat may need to be taken in a little lower than you can comfortably measure. If so, mark as low as you can and taper to seat curve when altering.

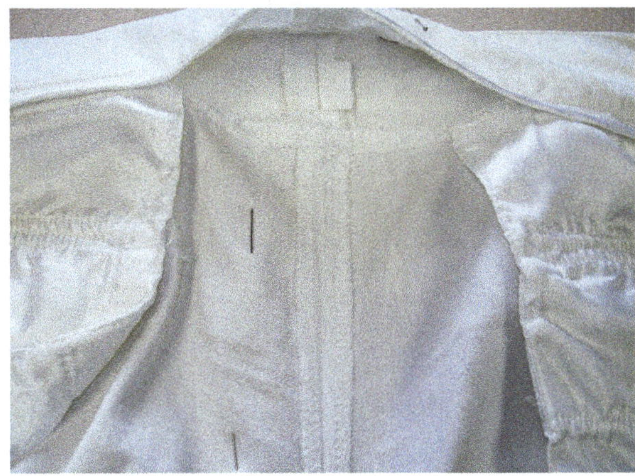

2. Chalk pins on wrong side below waistband. Measure amount at waist from pin to folded edge of fabric. Double and record that amount. Or chalk both sides of pin, unpin and measure, record that amount. Remove belt loop or loops in the center back. Open waistband stitching that is holding waistband facing to pant.

3. Yoke and/or waistband seams need to match. *Keep in mind that the presser foot may push the top fabric along.* With the bulkiness it can be challenging to get a good lay of the fabric at yoke or waistband seams. Pin seams together the amount from seat seam that needs to be taken in. Begin at waistband and stitch over waistband and yoke seams, stopping just below them. Remove fabric from machine and check to see if seams line up across from each other in the seat seam. If not, rip out stitches and try again. After seams are matching stitch entire seat seam making a smooth curve in crotch area or as marked. Stitch entire seat seam again over original stitching to make a strong seam.

4. If the seam was taken in much, it will need to be trimmed. As a general guide, a 1½" seam on each side of the waistband is a good amount. Tapering from there to a ½" seam in the curve of the seat is a good amount or duplicate as original. Some pants have a smaller seam with topstitching. *If the seam*

lays flat you may want to leave a larger seam for possible letting out in the future. Finish edge of seam as original with serging or seam tape.

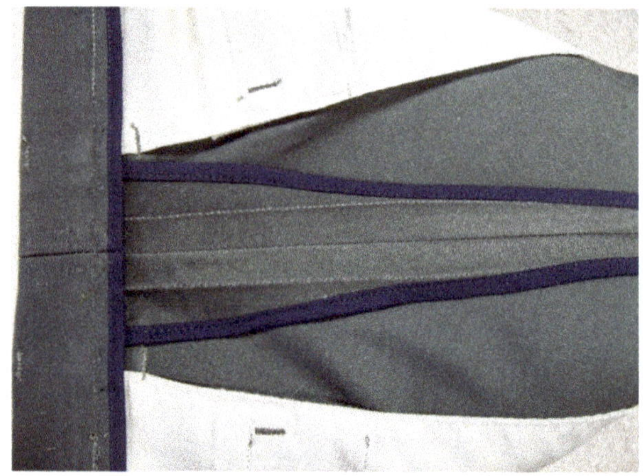

5. Press seam open if it was originally done that way. Top stitch if it was originally done that way.

6. Turn waistband seams under so that the serged corner is at seam forming a triangle. From inside of the waistband facing, machine stitch across the folded seams to hold it in place and to make a flat waistband.

7. Waistband facing can be secured by stitching in the ditch from right side beginning a couple inches away from the seamline and ending a couple inches from the seamline or as works best.

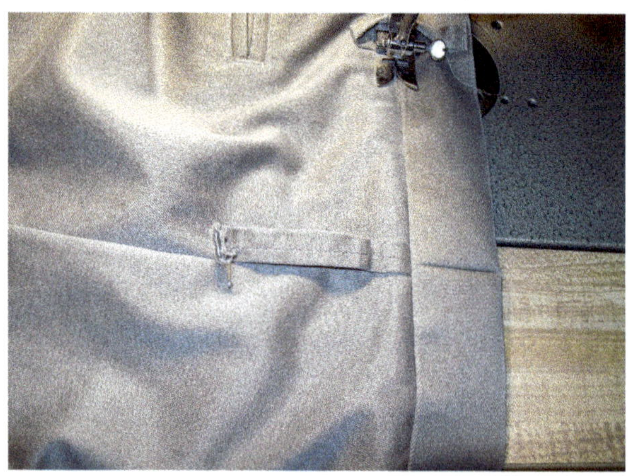

8. Reattach belt loop or loops as original.

9. Press.

Men's Trouser Waist Out

Trousers may or may not be able to be let out, it depends on how much fabric is in the center back seam. Most new trousers have enough fabric to let them out around 2". Check before or after the fitting to see if there is enough fabric while the customer is still there. To check, detach tacking holding the waistband down at the center back or, if able, pull out the facing. There must be at least ½ of the amount to be let out of the seam plus ¼" minimum (for the seam) on each side at the top of the waistband seam to let them out.

To fit for the amount to be let out: Have customer unbutton and unzip (at least ½ way down) trousers when on. Be professional, be quick, but be accurate. With a ruler, measure the amount from button to ¼" inside of buttonhole when held comfortably at waistband. This is the amount to be let out at waist. Record amount. Mark trousers at back of waistband vertically with two pins the distance apart the amount to be let out. Then place a pin horizontally. This means to let trousers out this amount. Go down to middle of zipper, measure amount from zipper side to zipper side. You may be able to visually determine this amount. Record amount. Place a horizontal pin in the center back seam at location to stop letting slacks out or record location. Mens trousers usually have more room through hips so usual requests will be for letting out waist, tapering through seat area. When altering, I would let them out at the waist and make a line to the curve of the seat tapering them to the original seam there or before that, as needed. If waist needs to be let out 1 ½" and trousers fit fine at bottom of zipper, I would just write on invoice to let trousers out 1 ½" tapering through seat.

1. Detach waistband facing at center back. Detach center back belt loop or two by center back (if applicable).

2. Place pins to hold the seat seam straight across at yoke and waist band seams in the area you will sew the new seam. Leave pins in until sewing to them. Use caution not to hit a pin with the needle. Leaving them into hold trouser seams together is accurate, but, I suggest you hand wheel over them, and go slow. Or remove them as you get to them.

3. Mark ½ of the amount to be let out at the top of trouser waistband wrong side. If trousers are to be let out 1 ½" the new seam would be ¾" over from the original seam, in the extra seam fabric. Remove pins just before stitching over seams or hand wheel stitches over the seams. Starting at the waistband seam, (not the top edge of pants) stitch over chalked spot to the top edge of pants, turn pants and stitch over your stitches to the waistband seam.

Continue sewing down to next seam, if there is one. Then, continue stitching, making a straight taper as needed to original seam. Overlap stitching in seam 1" or so. Cut threads. Examine seam. Waistband seams should be across from each other. Seat seam should be pretty straight. If satisfactory, stitch over first stitching so there are 2 rows of stitching in the new seat seam.

4.   Remove original stitching. Press seam open through waistband.

5.   Turn waist band seams under so that the serged corner is at seam forming a triangle. From inside of the waistband facing, machine stitch across the folded seams to hold it in place and to make a flat waistband.

6.   Waistband facing can be secured by stitching in the ditch from the right side through the whole seat seam and more if needed.

7.   Reattach belt loop or loops as original.

8.   Press

MEN'S WAIST IN OR OUT WITH ELASTIC WAISTBAND

Take in waist or let out following directions for trouser waist except that the facing does not open up. Starting at 1" below where alteration begins in seat seam, overlap stitching and stitch as marked through seat. Stitch waistband facing with trouser fabric as originally sewn following chalk lines. Backstitch at waist. Remove trousers from the machine. If seams match up well, restitch so there are 2 rows of stitching throughout new seat seam. Press seam open and flat. Tack at ends of waistband facing as original.

Men's Dress Slack Thigh In

Sides can be taken in on the outseam or on the inseam or both. If the slacks are too big above the crotch area, probably taking them in on the outseam is best. If slacks are too low through the crotch they will need to be taken in at the inseam. If they need to be taken in between the hip and hem they could be taken in on the inseam or the outseam or both if the amount is substantial. If outseam and inseam are both being taken in, ideally they should be taken in an equal amount. If the crotch is taken up through the inseam, taking the inseam in through the thigh and down may be the best option. Try to create a smooth line on slacks. They should lay flat on outseam and inseam if possible. Some people have different size hips and each side may need to be marked and taken in that amount.

To mark the crotch up, grasp the seat seam and pinch together the amount to be taken up and place a pin holding that amount. Just below the crotch, in the center back pant leg, grasp amount to be taken in through the leg and place a pin vertically. Place additional pins 3-4" apart down center back of leg with the amount needed to be taken in. You may be able to stop at knee area, at calf area, or you may need to go all the way down through the hem. *The amount to be taken in at the top of the inseam will need to match the amount taken in at the crotch (pinned in at the seat).* Mens dress slacks are designed to be taken in at the thigh. Usually the amount to be taken in should come out of the back of the slacks. If a large amount is to be taken in, you may need to take some out of the front of slack also. The crotch is cut shorter in the front with excess in the back, that is why all or most fabric should be taken out of the back. When marking for alteration, point pins the angle needed to taper. A pin placed horizontally will signify where to start or stop taking in. For a more accurate fitting, pin both legs.

1. Average pinned amount on each side if customer is even. If the customer doesn't know, ask if they have noticed slacks' different lengths on their legs in the past, if not, assume they are even.

2. Chalk on fabric on each side of pins on wrong side of slacks. Using wax chalk may leave marks when pressed on light colored or light weight fabric. Using clay chalk may leave marking that is hard to remove. The key is to mark so it can be seen but not leave a permanent mark. Usually we used wax chalk, but on delicate fabrics white clay chalk or pin marking worked best. Remove pins. *Hint: If side through pockets need to be token in you may need to take pockets apart and move them over the amount to be taken in, if the pocket edge lays along the side seam. This requires a lot more time to do the alteration. Look for this while fitting so you can let the customer know the price will reflect this.*

This is a case to alter one side at a time, to be able to, refer to and put the taken in side back with the same construction as the original. To take pants in at pockets, the pocket would need to be detached, the amount to be taken in cut off pant, and then the pocket reattached as original. Doing one side at a time will allow you to use the other one to refer to if there is a question.

If the pocket is slanted and side needs to be taken in at that area usually taking the seam in and narrowing the pocket opening works okay. If the opening is too short to be able to comfortably slide a hand in the pocket, you will need to reslant the pocket opening to make it longer.

Remove pins. Measure the amount between chalk lines. This is the total amount to be taken in. Parallel to this marking, place a pin this amount away from the previous seam on the right side back pant leg. The line should be pretty straight, no major ins or outs tapering smoothly at the end or through the hem.

3. Place right side of slack front crotch seamline over pin on back of slack crotch. Pin. Holding fabric taunt, evenly distribute and place a pin in the center between the crotch pin and where the taper stops or at hem with the front seamline over pin. Continue down leg placing the front seamline over pins on back of slacks. Taking slack thigh in to the knee area is enough to get a desired fit many times. A full leg taper may need to be done on slacks needing more taken in. Fabric will need to be distributed evenly between crotch and where the taper stops. Stitch along chalk lines making sure seam is relatively straight. If the seam lays good, restitch over original stitching from knee to crotch. Press seam either open or to the back of the slacks as the original.

4. Trim seam to original width or just a little wider. Serge edge.

5. If slacks had a crease in the center front or center back it may need to be moved. If so, press out old crease from the wrong side of slacks first. Use an even combination of vinegar and water in a spray bottle to aid in removing old crease lines as you press *Some slacks have permanent crease lines and will not be moveable. This is something that is good to establish at the fitting if possible to alert the customer to. If slacks are new and have tags that say permanent crease or similar wording, you probably will not be able to move it over.* On the ironing board, right side out, lay slacks with the hemline even and inseam and outseam laying one on top of the other. Some fabrics such as polyester, will need to be pressed using a press cloth. If unsure, use one, to avoid leaving a shiny finish on fabric. Press and steam edge of leg to form a new crease beginning at knee area, or where leg taper stopped. A pounding block will make a crisper crease. To use the pounding block, (instructions of page 4)

steam edge of slacks, clap pounding block immediately over edge to block steam in. Moving iron and lifting block just a bit, move along to lower edge of slack. Repeat on other edge of leg. Move slacks to edge of board with the knee area on side closest to you and crotch away from you. Starting at knee area, or where leg taper stopped, move up, steaming, clapping block on steam and continuing up along edge parallel to crotch. If slacks are pleated in front, the crease will need to line up with the pleat. If a lot was taken in, keeping the front crease looking good/pretty straight may not allow seams to line up one over the other near the crotch area. The front crease looking good/pretty straight takes precedence in that case. If there is no pleat, stop crease at crotch.

MEN'S DRESS SLACK THIGH OUT

Most mens dress slacks have a wide seam in the inseam through the thigh area on the back slack piece that can be let out. Seams are back to normal size at the knee area. When you let out the thigh all the way to the top or the crotch seam, the crotch seam is let out or lowered also. If the crotch seam does not need to be let out or lowered, the inseam can be tapered to the original seam at the crotch. Usually you would let out the inseam through the thigh area all the way to the top or crotch. There is not a good fitting method for this. It is an experienced guess. If a lot is needed, let it all out. If not much is needed, you may not need to let it all out. Determine how far down on slacks they need to be let out. A second fitting to see if the first alteration is accurate may be needed. If this is the case, stitch the inseam as you feel is correct. After the customer has approved, finish alteration.

1. Remove seam stitching on inseam, starting at the point the thigh needs to be let out through crotch or to ending spot. Open crotch seam up at top of inseam to release both seams.

2. With right sides together, pin inseam seams together at the top of the inseam, moving the front slack previous seam over (to make leg wider) on the back slack previous seam the amount to be let out. Slacks should be even at the top of the seam. *This can be a job that 3 hands work better than two. To get some help, what I would do sometimes, is to place pinned crotch seam under the presser foot. Put down, then hold slacks with the knee area away from machine getting an even distribution.* In center location, between the crotch, and where the alteration ends on the inseam, and with the front slack previous seamline over back slack previous seamline, move front slack seamline over the amount to be let out. Place a pin holding the front inseam on desired location on slack back, repeat until inseam is pinned every 3-4" or so.

If this is not enough to be let out to the desired thigh width, both sides can be let out as much as possible. If that is the case, starting at the knee area, overlap original stitching 1" below where seam is wider, taper to make a small seam just to the inside of the serging, skip # 3.

3. Overlap original stitching 1" below where the inseam will be let out. Stitching a pretty straight tapered seam, stitch in fold of slack front original seam all the way up inseam to crotch.

4. Examine to be sure seam is straight enough to lay flat when pressed open. Stitch again over first stitching. Backstitch at crotch seam.

5. Press seams open.

6. Restitch crotch seam as original.

7. If slacks had a crease in the center front or center back it may need to be moved. If so, press out old the crease from the wrong side of slacks first. Use an even combination of vinegar and water in a spray bottle to aid in removing old crease lines as you press. *Some slacks have permanent crease lines and will not be moveable. This is something that is good to establish at the fitting if possible to alert the customer to. If slacks are new and have tags that say permanent crease or similar wording you will probably have trouble moving it over. Some fabrics will need a press cloth over the fabric. If in doubt, use one.* To make a new crease, on the ironing board, lay slacks with the hem even at the bottom and the inseam laying over the outseam. Begin pressing crease where the tapering ended, using steam. Clap pounding block immediately over the slack edge, to block the steam in. After 5 seconds, remove block and repeat process where new crease stopped. Continue to crotch area. If pants are pleated in front at the waist, the crease will need to go to the pleat. Give preference to front crease looking straight when lining up with pleat and front crease. The inseam laying directly over the outseam at the crotch area, may need to be tweaked just a bit, to have the front crease be straight, if slacks were taken in a lot. See how they look when you hold them at the waistband and the crease falls as it is. If a lot was taken in, keeping the front crease looking good/pretty straight may not allow seams to line up one over the other near the crotch area. The front crease looking good/pretty straight takes precedence in that case. If there is no pleat, stop crease at crotch.

CHAPTER 3
JEANS

Sewing on denim requires a heavy duty needle, I used size 18. I also tried to duplicate the weight of thread used originally. If using heavy weight thread, machine tensions need to be changed. Sometimes a manufacturer would use a couple of threads at the same time. This could be duplicated by having two spools of thread threaded on top of machine and both threaded through the needle. The seam would need to be stitched on the outside in order for the thread combination to be visible. If a color match in heavy duty is not available, to strengthen the thread or to make it bolder, use two threads at a time. To get even stitching over seams use a wedge or another presserfoot lifter, or make apiece of fabric tripled over to put under the presserfoot at the beginning/ ending of stitching over the seam. Match stitch length to original hem stitch length.

Popular ⅝" Hem

1. Cut jean to be 1 ⅛" longer than finish line pin. To be sure the seam fold is correct place a line of pins along the finish line.

2. Turn under ½" and turn that again (finish line pin should be on edge).

3. Start on inseam, use a wedge before each seam, stitch near inside fold (away from bottom edge), with heavy duty thread with a #18 or heavy duty needle. Match stitch length to original hem stitch length.

4. Overlap stitching about an inch.

5. Press from inside first, then touch up outside as needed.

Reattaching Original Hem

After fitting for shortening jeans (with the original hem being reattached) I would suggest safety pinning a small note of paper to the hem stating "Reattach original hem". It is a little bit of insurance that the hem will be altered correctly.

1. Average amount to be shortened, record on paper.

2. Hand cut off ⅜" above old stitching on hem, pinning cut off to top of pant leg so there is no mix-up of what cut off goes to what leg.

3. Subtract ½" from total to be shortened. *This is for the ¼" seams.*

4. Cut off that amount from bottom edge of pant leg.

5. Line up original hem piece on bottom of respective pant leg making sure seams match (machine baste each side seam first to save ripping time).

6. With right sides together, stitch with a ¼" seam using thread color that closely matches denim.

7. Zigzag seam with short stitch length slightly under ¼" width zigzag. Carefully trim closely all frayed threads using caution not to cut zigzag thread.

8. Top stitch seam on outside just above seam with seam turned away from hem.

9. Press.

Waist and Seat In

To make an accurate fitting, strong pins need to be used. T-pins are what I liked to use, especially for the waist. Starting at the waistband, pinch fabric in and place a pin in the waistband to desired amount per customer. Going down the seat seam, pinch fabric in and pin until the fabric lays smooth on seat area and in proportion to above pins. *The seat seam is bulky, I would make it easier to pinch, pin, and mark the amount to be taken in by doing it at the side of the seat seam.* Continue until you either cannot reach any farther in seat area or jeans fit at that area. If the seat seam fits at that area, place a pin horizontally to indicate where to stop taking seam in.

Some manufacturers use multiple colors of thread, on one pair of jeans, duplicate as original.

1. On wrong side of jeans, chalk pins well on each side of the pin. Remove pins. If chalk does not show up well a straight or safety pin can be used to mark also. *This will be the amount to be taken in at that spot.* Remove belt loop if there is one. Remove labels on inside of waistband if there are any. At center back, open waistband stitching on top and bottom edges about 2" more each side than the amount to be taken in. Sometimes a label is sewn on the waistband that may restrict this. If so, you can try to open up less stopping about ½" away from label (to allow secure stitching on waistband when putting stitching back), or you may need to remove the label some to get into waistband. Measure and record the amount to be taken in at the waistband. Cut waistband straight down at center back using location of back belt loop and center of center back seam for a guide. A center back seam will be made in the waistband measuring ½ of the amount recorded to be taken in (seam will measure ½ of the amount but since it will be taken in each side, the actual amount taken in will be that amount doubled).

2. In the seat area, measure amount to be taken in. Parallel to that spot, place a pin ½ of that amount from the folded edge of the flat felled seam. Place one pin on outside of jeans and one pin on inside of jeans each side over, from the folded under seam. Remove seat seam stitching from waist to about 1" below stop pin. This is usually a chain that will pull from the waist. If so, break the thread chain (in a loop) with a ripper in seam about 1" below stop pin before you start to pull the thread. **This is crucial to stop the chain.**

Stopping below the stop point allows a smooth transition from original to altered area. To remove the chain stitch, cut top thread tail at waist and pull a thread at a time from the inside of jeans until one pulls the chain. This will take some practice to get the right one but it is worth it when you master it. When done, check that no loop in chain is sticking out and chain is stopped.

3. Fold and press denim along pin line in the direction of original fold, tapering to end of area to be taken in at stop pin.

4. Cut off excess denim leaving ⅜" or original seam amount over from fold or pin. Remove pins.

5. Practice stitching over original stitching in seat area with no thread in machine to get stitch length matching original or with thread in using the hand wheel at 1" below where stitching is stopped; check each stitch and adjust until needle enters fabric at same location over the original stitches. With flat felled seam snuggly folded together similar to original, begin stitching up seat seam on left side of seam.

Matching the yoke seem is important and tricky to do. Continually check location of yoke seams for even placement, and for the flat felled seam to be snuggly folded together, continue stitching up seam. Keep in mind that the presser foot will probably push the top yoke denim a little bit so ideally top yoke seam should be just short of being across the lower denim yoke seam. At about ½" below yoke seem stop with needle in denim. Place wedge under presser foot

Stitch over yoke keeping yoke stitching across from each other. Continue stitching to end of seat seam. Check to be sure seam is evenly folded/stitched under seam. If so, starting at 1" below where stitching was stopped, sew up the right side of the flat felled seam, making sure seam is folded flat underneath, using wedge at yoke seam. Try to keep stitching straight and parallel to first stitch line.

6. Mark ½ of the amount to be taken in at waistband with a pin at both edges and at top fold line of waistband on one side. Line up cut edges with right sides together. Placing side up with pins designating the amount to be taken in, put the needle down into waistband at top edge fold lines placing at pin (then remove pin), and stitch to end. Remove from machine and check for fold lines to match up. If they look good, restitch over original stitching and over fold line to the other end, backstitch. Beginning about ½" over previous stitching stitch through fold line and to other end, backstitch. Turn waistband right side out and tuck back of pants inside it. Waistband and seat seam should lay flat. Trim waistband seam to ½". Press open.

7. If there were labels stitched to inside of waistband, sew these back as original.
8. Stitch top waistband row of stitching overlapping original stitching about 1" at start and stop, making sure all lays flat.
9. If a belt loop was inserted into the waistband tack it as original over seat seam.
10. Keeping all labels free, stitch bottom waistband seam overlapping original stitching on both sides if able to.
11. Sew belt loops back as original.
12. Press

BELT LOOPS

Generally 5 Belt loops are attached, center back flush with top of waistband, generally around 2 ⅜" to back of side seams, and generally around 3 ½" from center front. Depending on the size, this may need to be adjusted. To attach, a narrow zigzag stitch is usually used. Heavy duty thread may or may not be used. Match original stitching thread color and weight if possible. Place a wedge under presser foot and next to belt loop to keep stitch quality more uniform. Begin near end of top edge of loop, as in photo. Duplicate stitching as on other loops. Usually the stitching ends shy of the end of the loop. Backstitch a couple stitches and then stitch across belt loop, almost to the end of top edge, then backstitch a couple stitches. To hold the loop in place better, stitching a straight stitch first may be desired.

To construct a new belt loop, cut a denim piece 3" x 1 ¼". Serge one long edge. Fold raw edge side under ⅜", then fold serged edge over that so the width is ½". Stitch down the side just catching the edge of the serged edge. Stitch down the other side the same distance from the edge. Or duplicate stitching as was originally done.

Flat Felled Seam Leg Taper

Pin the amount of the pant leg to be taken in. Jeans can often be taken in on one side only of each leg and still hang okay. If the amount to be taken in is too much to accommodate by taking in only on one side, the amount to be taken in will need to be taken in ½ of the amount on each side of the pant leg. The following instructions are for taking in one side of jeans with a flat felled seam. The amount to be taken in will be done ½ of the amount on each side of the flat felled seam.

1. On wrong side of pant leg, chalk pins on each side of the pin. *This will be the amount to be taken in at that spot.*

2. Measure amount to be taken in. Parallel to that spot, piece a pin ½ of that amount from the folded under edge of the flat felled seam on each side of the seam (placing one pin on outside of jeans, and one pin on inside of jeans on the side of seam fold).

3. Fold denim along pin line in the direction of original turned under fabric so pins line up on pressed edge, tapering to end of area to be taken in at stop pin.

4. Cut off denim leaving ⅜" or original seam amount on seam side of flat felled seam pin.

5. Line pant leg up on flat surface with the top and bottom even. With the pant fabric evenly distributed between the top and bottom on outside of jeans place pins or drawn a line with chalk parallel to hemline across from each other as a guide for assuring that you are getting a even feed of fabric as the seam is sewn.

    It is very difficult on a full leg taper or a long leg taper to get this even without this method since when you are stitching the seam, the pant leg is not laying flat, and you cannot monitor this without markers.

6. Place flat felled seam together as original seam was, butting seam together with fold interlapping; stitch seam beginning about 1" above where stitching ended. Use same length stitch and similar thread color and weight if possible. Be sure thread tension is correct.

7. Stitch other side of flat felled seam. This can be done from the right side up or from the wrong side up. From the top gives you more even stitches. All must be lined up just right to assure success in your seam.

8. Resew hem if needed, stitching from right side to make sure stitch lines match up. Press.

Regular Seam Leg Taper

Pin amount to be tapered in along side seam with customer's approval. Pins should be placed no more than 4" or so apart. Place a pin across at the point to stop and/or start the taper.

1. Inside jeans, chalk each side of seam with fabric held open at the pin. Measure amount between chalk marks and mark ½ of the total amount to be taken in on one side of the seam with a pin parallel to the side seam.

2. Stitch seam amount at pins.

3. Trim seam to width of original seam and serge. Press toward back of jean leg, or as original.

4. Resew hem if needed, stitching from outside to make sure stitch lines match up. Press.

FRONT POCKET REPLACEMENT

1. *In most cases I did not need to cut out the entire pocket to replace it. Examine pocket for worn areas. This is an area that is challenging to get into, and if only the bottom of pocket is damaged, and if the customer approves, you can replace that part only.*

2. Cut off the damaged area of pocket at the area where the fabric is stable enough to be securely stitched with the new fabric.

3. Cut a replacement pocket (there is specific pocket fabric available from wholesalers but there are other types of fabric similar to the original fabric that would work) using the cut off pocket for a pattern but adding 1" more fabric to top of pocket on side that will be attached to the pants.

4. Open pocket seam stitching about ½" above where original pocket was cut off.

Pin new pocket bottom to pocket. With right sides together, pin new pocket bottom to original pocket; beginning at the center (where the folded edge of the pocket is) and to the curved seam of the pocket. Attach in a ½" seam. Serge seam. Topstitch seam down through seam. Inside of the pocket should be smooth with the actual seam on the outside of the pocket. Turn pocket inside out. Starting at side seam overlap stitching or backstitch and stitch a scant ¼" seam rounding to end where folded, backstitch. Trim seam to a secure ⅛" seam. Push pocket right side out. With seam laying out flat restitch it with just over ¼" seam. Turn pocket inside out. Trim any raw edges that show.

For Jean zipper replacement instructions go to zippers chapter 7.

For Jean patches instructions go to patch chapter 8.

CHAPTER 4

SHIRTS AND BLOUSES

SHORTEN SHIRT LONG SLEEVES

To fit for the desired length, have the customer put the shirt on. Button cuffs. Pinch excess fabric up and pin along sleeve above cuff.

Have the customer reach with arms straight out and move around to check if the length is okay. If their arms are different lengths both sleeves will need to be marked. I recommend doing one sleeve at a time until you are comfortable doing this alteration. This way you can refer to the original application if needed.

1. Chalk top and bottom sides of pins on inside of shirt. *Using wax chalk may leave marks when pressed on light colored or light weight fabric. Using clay chalk may leave residue that is hard to remove. The key is to mark so it can be seen but not leave a permanent mark. Usually we used wax chalk, but on delicate fabrics white clay chalk or pin marking worked best.* Remove pins. Average between chalk marks. This is the amount that will need to be

shortened. Record this amount. Repeat if the other sleeve needs to be a different length, record amount. I would suggest safety pinning a small note of paper to the sleeve stating "Shorten at the hemline or cuff by removing the average amount pinned". It is a little bit of insurance that the hem will be altered correctly.

2. Detach cuff, only taking out the stitches holding the cuff to sleeve. Pin cuff to top of sleeve removed from, if altering both sleeves at this time.

3. Sleeve plackets are constructed different ways. I have given directions for some common applications used.

Placket Method 1, With a 1 piece long strip placket finished size ⅝" wide or so: Place a safety pin on side of placket on the outside of the shirt. Remove placket piece (notice design of stitching, such as a square, X, etc.), pin it on top of sleeve removed from, if doing both sleeves at this time. If there is a button/buttonhole, detach button but not buttonhole. If the buttonhole is stitched through to sleeve, trim sleeve along edge of buttonhole to detach. Cut off sleeve at bottom of sleeve the amount to be shortened. Extend slit up the exact amount to be shortened. The slit should be a straight line along the grain of fabric. Sometimes the top of the slit will be cut with a V. This method will lay nice upon replacing the placket. Duplicate original cut. With top edge of V of sleeve inserted inside the placket at center, stitch placket to the V slit, having safety pin side to the outside (remove safety pin). *V slits need to be just tucked inside, with raw edge inside but close to edge of placket.* Stitch seam with shirt tucked inside of placket as original seam amount. With the needle in fabric, turn shirt at sleeve slit, stitch to end of placket. The placket and sleeve raw edge should be close in length. Place the machine needle in the beginning stitches of the corner you just stitched, stitch across top edge of V again, turn at corner with needle in fabric and sleeve inserted in placket. Stitch to end of placket. The placket and sleeve raw edge should be close in length. No raw edge fabric at V should be outside of placket. Sleeve fabric should lay flat. Fold placket along original fold lines at the center (top of slit). Sides should be even at bottom. Stitch design along old stitch lines. Overlap stitching at end on one side to reinforce.

Proceed to attaching cuff directions.

Placket Method 2, With a 2 piece placket: Place a safety pin on side of placket on the outside of the shirt. Remove placket piece (notice design of stitching), pin placket on top of sleeve removed from, if doing both sleeves at this time. If there is a button/buttonhole, detach button but not buttonhole. If buttonhole is stitched through to sleeve trim sleeve along edge of buttonhole to detach. Cut off sleeve at bottom of sleeve the amount to be shortened. Cut slit up the exact amount the sleeve will be shortened. The slit should be a straight line along the grain of fabric. Sometimes the top of the slit will be cut with a V or a T. This will lay nice after replacing placket. Duplicate original cut.

The larger side of placket will be sewn over the other one. The narrower strip of fabric is folded under ¼" on each side folded one more time along the edge of the strip.

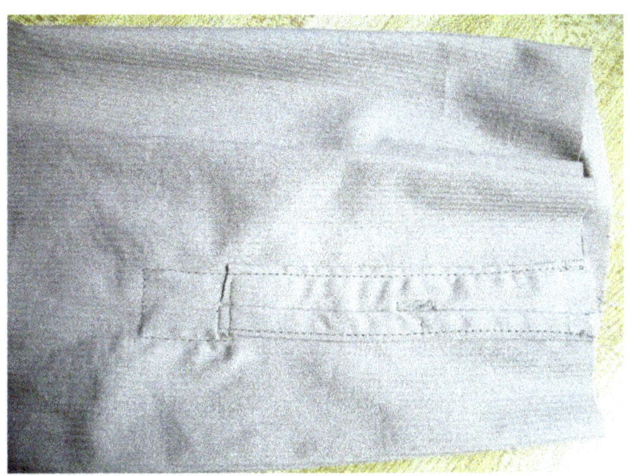

1. Surefire way to attach narrow strip, method 1: To catch the strip and have top stitching straight attach strip at first fold to back of sleeve slit, stitching inside of first fold of strip. Backstitch at start and end of seam. The width of seam should be about ¼" or as original. Fold strip as original and topstitch from outside. The topstitching should be covering the first stitch line.

    Quicker if it works, method 2: With strip folded as original, insert edge of sleeve slit into folded edge of narrow strip. Straight stitch along old stitch line, backstitching at both ends.

2. If a V was cut into the shirt sleeve, it will need to be tucked into the wider strip or attached at center back as original. Stitch across the wider strip where the top of slit is, stitching over original stitching. With shirt laying flat and strip folded as original, stitch up to top, pivot, and down to where stitching started.

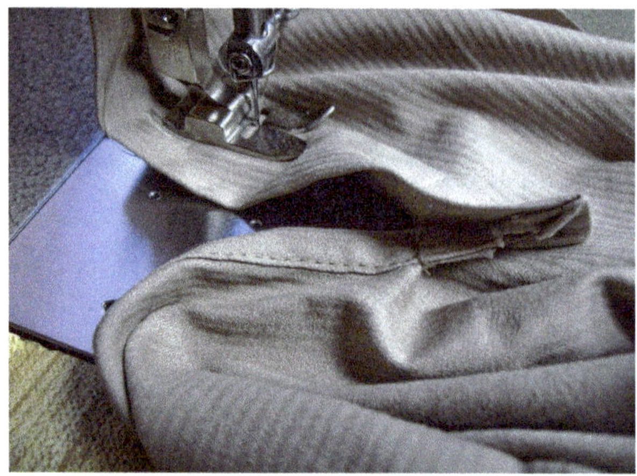

Strip should follow the straight grain of the fabric. Stitch across strip over previous stitching and stop at side of strip. Cut threads. Both sides of strip should be about the same length at hem.

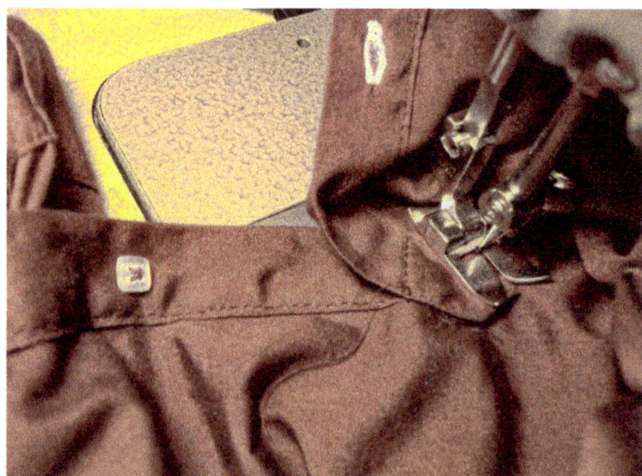

Placket Method 3, A narrow one piece strip about ¼" wide when finished:

1. *Sure fire way to attach narrow strip, method 1:* To catch the strip and have topstitching straight, attach strip at first fold to back of sleeve slit, stitching inside of first fold of slit, stitch inside of first fold of strip, with raw edges even. When stitching, continue holding raw edges even, opening sleeve slit so it will be straight and near to facing at raw edge. Backstitch at start and end of seam. The width of seam should be about ¼" or as original. Fold strip as original and top stitch from outside. The topstitching should be covering the first stitch line.

Quicker if it works, method 2: With strip folded as original, insert edge of sleeve slit into folded edge of narrow strip. Straight stitch along old stitch line, backstitching at both ends.

2. After the cuff has been attached to the sleeve, with the sleeve inside out, and with cuffs even, straight stitch beginning at top edge of slit through strip (at an angle towards cuff) folded edge, backstitch, straight stitch. This will hold the strip to the inside of the sleeve.

Attaching sleeve to cuff:

3. Sleeves may have 0-4 pleats at cuff. Look at original sleeve cut off. Pleats should be in the same general location and the same general amount. Using the original amount as a guide, if original sleeve was tucked inside cuff ½" the new amount tucked inside cuff should be ½". Place a pin (parallel to the bottom edge of the shirt) holding pleat/pleats the distance of original tucked inside seam of shirt sleeve. Be sure pleats are going the same direction they were originally. If so, place pins along entire bottom edge of shirt sleeve the amount

of seam, about ²" apart (this will be the place cuff should be lined up to). Make sure placket is even at pins. One side of placket may have been turned under. If so this will need to be duplicated, pin placket to underside. Bottom edge of sleeve with pleats pinned needs to be the same width as the top edge of the cuff. Tuck bottom edge of the shirt sleeve inside of cuff on button end of cuff. Cuff underside should be flat, laying straight. Start stitching over original stitch line about ½" from edge of cuff stitching towards edge. Stop with needle down at edge. Pivot and turn sleeve/cuff around. Stitch over original stitching slowly lining up cuff at pin line, checking cuff underside for straight placement.

Remove pins when you get almost to them. Check for sleeve width/cuff width lining up before last two pleats are stitched in. Adjust pleats as needed, backstitch ½" or so. If another row of stitching was originally sewn, duplicate it as so.

4. Line the second cuff up, with right sides together, over the completed cuff. Mark with a pin where pleats are. Adjust pleats if necessary Starting at

button end of cuff, stitch as on first sleeve making sure pleats match up to pins on cuff.

5.   Sew button on placket under buttonhole.

6.   Press.

MEN'S SHIRT SHORT SLEEVES LENGTH ADJUSTMENT

Fashions change as do the popular sleeve length but the measurements we used for average length from center back neck to finish line of sleeve were: XL 21 ½", L 20 ¾", M 20". Or you can mark the desired length of the sleeve. To mark desired short sleeve length on a long sleeve, horizontally put in a safety pin at the general area, fasten it and then gently press it into the customer's arm with your thumb until the desired length is determined.

1.   Line sleeve on rotary cutting grid laying sleeve seam on one side and outside sleeve fold along grid straight line.

2.   Cut sleeve off 1" longer than finish line safety pin. If the sleeve is tapered it may need to have the seam let out below finish line so it will lay flatter in hem. Resew sleeve seam over original stitching to 1" from cut bottom edge, taper towards serged edge so sleeve gets wider through hem.

3.   Serge edge of side seam, if let out. Serge bottom edge of sleeve.

4.   Pin up a 1" hem, distributing fullness of outside fabric, if not even. Pin at least 4 places, making sure fullness is even. Straight stitch hem ¾"-⅞" on top of the serging (determine which is best/most secure for the shirt) starting at seam with stitch length matching stitching in shirt. Overlap stitching about an inch.

5.   Press.

SHIRT TAPERING AT SIDES

Pin sides of shirt in the amount to be taken in. Depending on how large the shirt is you may need to take it in through the sleeves. Average the amount to be taken in on each side (it works good to lay shirt out on a flat surface, and line seams up next to each other). If seams are flat felled, place a pin ½ of the amount to be taken in on each side of fold of seam placing one pin on the outside of shirt and one on the inside of the sleeve, on side of seam fold. Cut off excess fabric on seam side of flat felled seam pin, allowing for amount in seam (usually between ¼" and ⅜"). Press under the amount to be folded under in the seam along pin line (be sure to press under in original seam direction, check at where seam is still together to be sure). Match stitch length with original stitch length in seam. Make sure seam is folding the direction original was. Fold flat felled seam snuggly together, similar to original, as you sew down the side of shirt. Stitch on folded edge of seam, beginning about 1" above where stitching has stopped, on outside of right side out shirt seam. It is easy to pull one side more than the other as folding and stitching. To guard against this, pins can be placed evenly at the same distance from the top/bottom of side seam.

When stitching line these pins up across from each other.

If shirt side seams are regular seams, place a pin with amount to be taken in from seam. These pins are marking where the finished seam will be. Open hem at side seams if the seam needs to be taken in through it. If tags are sewn into the seam they will need to be removed and sewn in the same area when the seam is sewn.

NARROW BLOUSE SHOULDERS

To have an accurate fitting, be sure the blouse is positioned evenly on customer specifically on each side of neck. Button the blouse to be sure things hang as they will when worn. If the customer has two different size shoulders (height, or width) each will need to be fit for narrowing. Most people have the same, for a more accurate fitting each should be marked and then averaged together. Mark the amount to be narrowed by pinching fabric above sleeve seam in the shoulder area and pin that amount together. Continue pinning down the front and back as needed (try to pin every 2" on both shoulders so the amounts can be averaged). Measure the amount pinned and average that amount at each place pinned on armhole. Such as, top pins at shoulder seam would be averaged, the next pin down in front on each side (placed at same area) would need to be averaged, then the next pin down, etc until all pins are averaged in front and back. If the blouse needs side seams taken in, in addition to narrowing the shoulder, this is another alteration. If so, see Dress Sides In, Chapter 5. If the side seam does not need to be taken in, it works well to stop taking in the armhole up to about an inch on each side of the side seam. This leaves enough room to leave the side seam alone and not have to put it back in and tapers out nicely on most items. Some will need the shoulders narrowed this far down. Others will not. Open the seam attaching sleeve to blouse beginning at 1" from side seam, up, around sleeve to 1" from side seam on other side. The seam will need to be put back as original construction. Mark both sides of the fabric pinned together on the inside of blouse with chalk. This is the amount to be narrowed. Cut the blouse fabric (beginning at the spot narrowing should begin) the amount between the chalk marks, up and around sleeve to other side with a pretty straight line tapering out to end.

If you cut the exact amount the shoulder needs to be narrowed, when the same width seam is put in, the shoulder should be the exact amount pinned narrower.

Hint: If the sleeve has gathering at the top of the sleeve (or if it is pleated), it will need to be basted with a long stitch for gathering or pleating in fullness (leave underarm flat, gathering or pleating only the area originally gathered or pleated), at seam line before aligning it up. The sleeve fabric will need to be distributed evenly when lining up to armhole opening. Establish the center of sleeve by folding it flat with underarm seam on one side. The other side when sleeve is flat is the center. Establish the center of the sleeve opening on the blouse by folding at the side seam and when flat the top is the center (this may or may not be at the shoulder seam if there is one). With right sides together, pin the center of the blouse sleeve opening with the center of the sleeve at seam lines. Pin underarm area together, lining up sleeve underarm seam with side seam. Align and pin the underarm area in the sleeve and blouse to the beginning of gathering, if there is any. Align and pin the rest of the sleeve, distributing gathering evenly or pleats as originally placed if there are any. Stitch arm hole in same width seam as original. Restitch sleeve seam ⅛" from first stitching in the seam for more strength. Serge edge of armhole seam. Topstitch or finish seam as original was. Press seam toward sleeve. If garment is lined the lining will need to be narrowed with the same method.

MAKING A T-SHIRT INTO A V-NECK

Mark desired center front bottom of V on customer with a safety pin.

1. With scissors next to original neck seam, cut ribbing off at back of shirt on shirt side of seam. With scissors next to original neck seam, cut through shoulder seam and along neck curve until you can make a straight cut to ⅜" above bottom of the V. Cut other side the same.

2. Serge cut edge of t-shirt. Stretch serging along neck edge to be sure tension is loose enough not to break when stretched.

3. *I found I preferred not to pin this but to turn and hold as I sewed.* At center back of neck fold fabric under ½". If there is a tag for the center back, baste in place or insert that now. From center back, topstitch with double needle ⅜" from edge (to catch hem and leave a little extra). As you stitch from the outside, and have fabric folded under, feel for the edge of the hem as you sew, making sure you are catching it, and it is where it should be. Stretch fabric a little as you sew to allow for thread to stretch when worn, if needed. Continue to turn under ½" as you sew, keeping outside and turned under fabric even (shoulder seams should be straight through both). From the shoulder seam to bottom of the V turn under will need to be stretched a little more then the t-shirt outside. Sew straight to the bottom of the V. At V try to turn in a V shape (double needle will not pivot) and go back up to the shoulder seam turning under ½" as you sew, keeping outside and turned under fabric even, or stretch turned under fabric a little, if needed, to align nicely. Stitch back to center back, overlapping stitching 1" or so.

4. Lightly press and steam. T-shirt should shrink into a V-neck shape.

Shorten a T-Shirt

Pin t-shirt up for customer to desired finished length. Move all pins to the fold (the desired finish length). Average pins. Line t-shirt straight on a grid (many t-shirts are not cut straight). Cut a straight line below the pinned finish line, the original hem length plus ⅛". For example, if the original hem length was ⅞" wide, cut a straight line 1" below the finish line pin. This method can also be used to shorten t-shirt sleeves, as the photo shows the straight edge of sleeve lined up below.

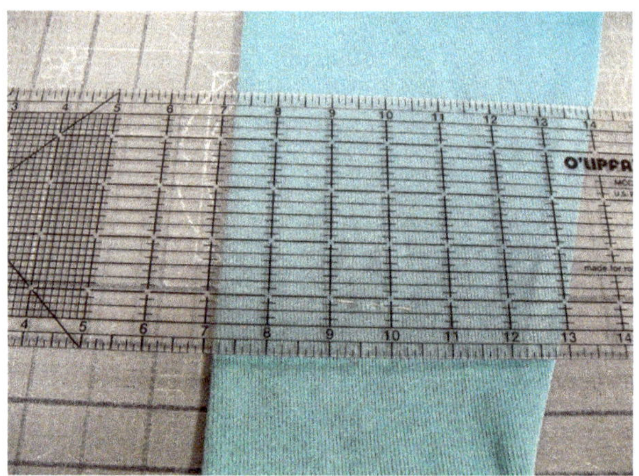

1. Serge cut edge.

2. Pin hem up amount to finish line pin placing pins near fold (this allows room for the presser foot at the end of the hem). Continue pinning hem up the entire width of the hem placing pins about 2" apart and near the fold.

3. Place garment on machine right side up. See double needle hem image on page 30. Using a double needle and matching threads, at the side seam, begin stitching hem the width of the original hem from the outside of the shirt. This will allow for ⅛" extra in hem. Using a guide on your machine bed may aid you in stitching straight. Stretch the hem slightly when stitching to allow thread some room to stretch when t-shirt is worn.

4. Lightly press and steam. Hem should not wave. Spray with vinegar water and re-steam/press if needed to get a flatter hem.

Shorten Sweater Sleeves or Sleeves with a Ribbing

Mark length of sleeve by pinching amount of fabric to be shortened, and pin that amount above the ribbing. After fitting for shortening sleeves with the original ribbing being reattached, I would suggest safety pinning a small note of paper to the hem stating "Reattach original hem". It is a little bit of insurance that the hem will be altered correctly.

1. Average amount to be shortened, record on paper.
2. With scissors, cut ribbing off ⅜" above where it ends (this excess will be in the seam, allowing altered cuff to have the same as original amount in the ribbing). Try not to agitate the cut edge. It will fray.
3. Subtract ½" from the total to be shortened.
4. Cut off that amount from raw edge of sleeve bottom.
5. Line up original hem piece on bottom of sleeve making sure seams match (machine baste first to save ripping time).
6. With right sides together, stitch with a ¼" seam using thread color that closely matches garment.
7. Serge seam.
8. Topstitch seam on outside (with seam facing towards sleeve) close to seam. If seam is wavy, you can gather it in a bit by stitching again over stitches with a larger stitch and using elastic thread in the bobbin. Be sure to secure the ends of the elastic thread so it doesn't ravel. This can be done by backstitching or hand stitching the ends down.
9. Steam and lightly press. Press into shape. If seam is wavy, spray with vinegar water, steam, repeat as necessary.

CHAPTER 5

DRESSES AND SKIRTS

DRESS OR SKIRT SHORTENING

Dress shortening methods are similar to slacks shortening. Generally a 1½" hem is a good amount. If the manufacturer has chosen a different amount it could be for a good reason. Or it could be just to save fabric. Personally, I prefer to leave at least a 1½" hem in most dresses and skirts. Generally wool garments have a larger hem. If the original hem is more than 1½", I would put that back in. If the original hem was finished with hem tape, I would do that again. Using hem tape helps the hem hang better. Some garments will hang with the hem parallel to the floor. Some garments will hang uneven. Let's face it, people are not straight as a board. We have bumps, bulges, etc. To get a straight hem even from the floor a skirt marker should be used. Or you can measure an even line from the floor with a yard stick. Place a pin horizontally at the same measurement from the floor all the way around the garment about 3-4" apart at the desired length. This is the finish line. Sometimes a customer would bring a skirt in and request that we shorten it a certain amount. We would then ask, is it even? If they would respond, "yes", we would just do it evenly from original hem as requested. We were always willing to measure to be sure of an even finished hem from the floor.

1. Cut off 1 ½" longer than finish line or amount of original hem (if bottom edge is tapered, hem should be small enough to lay smooth).

2. Serge edge turning side seams towards garment back or as original. If hem tape was used on the original hem it needs to be removed and reused (if in good condition). If it is not in good condition, replace it with similar hem tape. If bottom edge of garment gets wider or if it is shortened a bunch

you may need to add more hem tape to go around the complete garment. If you try to make it fit and it is too short, you may end up with a gathered looking hem. Sew hem tape on with plenty of give.

3. Pin up 1 ½" hem or as original, lining up side seams and center front and center back, distributing evenly any discrepancy between hem and garment width so hem lays flat. Blindstitch at edge of serging, catching edge of hem. *Do a quality check to be sure all stitches catch and that they are not too deep. I found that if you adjust the stitch to where it is not catching on all stitches and then adjust just a little until they are all caught you are in the right depth. You may need to press hem to be sure how hem will look after pressing. If stitches show too much and blindstitcher is dialed down as much as possible to just catch fabric, hem may need to be put in by hand.* Monitor stitch depth as you stitch. After stitching the whole way around the garment, overlap stitching an inch or two. Cut thread, cutting in the loop so it will not pull out if pulled on. A good quality hem may need to be done more than once to make sure stitch depth is at the correct adjustment.

4. Press using a bit of steam from the inside first and then from the outside using only enough pressure to lay hem flat.

Dress or Skirt Lengthening
follow methods used
on Slacks and Pants Lengthening

DRESS OR SKIRT WITH A SLIT

If there is a vent or slit in the hem of the garment, it will have to be finished as close to possible to the original. Pay special attention to this to be sure to get both sides of the slit even. Mark hemline with a pin on each side exactly opposite each other. Fold garment at hem with right sides together with pin being at the bottom edge. Do not stitch over pin, removing it just before getting to it. Stitch slit seam, backstitching at hemline (make sure the hem is laying flat) with finish line on bottom edge, and up to the end of the hem/slit, backstitch. Turn right side out. Garment should lay flat with the hem at bottom edge. Repeat on the other side.

VENT TYPE SLIT: Some slits are more like a jacket vent and will have a different application. One side will be stitched like a slit, the other side will be stitched together at the finish line.

If so, chalk finish line on the wrong side. With right sides together and with fold of slit on edge, all laying even, stitch along chalked finish line from fold to end of facing. Backstitch both ends. Turn right side out. Garment should lay flat with seam along the bottom edge. Duplicate original finish of hem and top stitch if it was originally. Press.

Lined Dress or Skirt Shortening

Shorten outside layer to length pinned with a blind stitched hem or as original hem. Lining length is measured off of the outside fabric in most cases. The exception would be when the dress/skirt is stretchy, and stretches when the garment is worn. Then the lining would need to be pinned to outside fabric along hemline (every 3-4") when it is on the customer.

To shorten lining as outside garment: open dress or skirt on the ironing board, with lining next to the board, and skirt fabric on the outside. Place side seams together. Gently tug on lining and outside fabric until both relax. Place a pin holding both together near bottom of garment. Repeat at other side seam. Repeat at center front and back. Continue until garment is pinned along hem every 3-4". This is to assure lining will be the correct length. Cut lining to be ½" longer than finished dress/skirt. Press lining under ½". Turn that under 1" and straight stitch hem. Finished lining length should be 1" shorter than dress/skirt. Connectors can be used to keep lining in place at side seams. If the manufacturer has used them we put them back in if they are usable, if not, we make some by serging a length of thread about 2" long at the seams near the hem to hold side seams and center back seams in position. See image on page 24. Lightly press from inside first then lightly press from outside.

Dress Sides In

To fit sides in on a dress begin at the top of the area needed to take in. For example, if the complete dress is too large, taking it in through the center back seam would be easiest but that would shift all fabric to back somewhat. Check the sleeves, side seams, etc. to see if they look tweaked to the back. Armholes still need to be centered at arms. Taking the dress in at sides would be more proportioned. Does the dress fit well above the bottom of the armhole? If it is too big, taking the sleeves out and narrowing the shoulders would be an option. It involves a lot of work, hence expense, so it may not be feasible. If the dress needs to be taken in at the bustline and lower, start the taper by placing a pin across at the side seam to show where to start, then, slant pins just as the seam needs to be sewn. *A smooth finished seam (when the garment is on) can only be achieved if the fitting is precise.* Place additional pins about 2-4" apart, (with pins holding extra fabric to be taken in) go down garment to the ending spot or through hem as needed. If you start or end in the seam and not at the top or hem of it, the taken in seam must be very gradual so it will lay smooth. Repeat for opposite side seam. If the dress has princess seams that extend above the bottom of the armholes and you need to take dress in a little higher, you may want to take that seam in instead of the side seam. If there is a lot to be taken in, you may have to take in more seams to distribute the amount taken in. If too much is taken in through one or two seams, the finished garment may not lay good. Much will depend on the size, and cut of the garment. If the dress is sleeveless or strapless, taking it in the center back may be a good option. Have the customer look at the garment after fitting it, and point out potential out of proportion problems and available options to the customer. Sometimes front or back darts can be taken in to take some fabric out in the waist area. Use much caution doing this though, because if they are taken in too much, they will not lay good, and can leave fabric above or below dart with an excess, a fabric bump. Extending darts down through hem can be an option also.

1. Average pins of opposite seams to be taken in such as side seams, front princess seams, back princess seams, front darts, or back darts. Chalk wrong side of garment on both sides of pin. Remove pins.

2. Stitch over chalk lines beginning or ending gradually if starting in the middle of a seam/dart so it will lay flat.

3. Trim seam to original width or a little larger if it will lay flat. Serge edge of seam.

4. Press seam to back or as original.

SLEEVELESS DRESS SHOULDERS UP

This alteration is commonly done to bring up the armholes when the armholes are too low. It may or may not be the appropriate alteration for every client, depending on where the bust fits. If there are darts, princess seams, etc. that fit correctly to the bust you should not bring up the shoulders. Pin shoulder seams up the amount desired and check this. Don't assume the shoulder seam should be brought up evenly, the inside of the shoulder could be less or more. Pin accurately. Enough room under arms should be left for comfort. If the armholes are just below arms they may irritate underarm area.

1. Detach armhole facing and/or lining from sleeve at top. If the shoulder seam needs to be brought up through the neck seam, detach that side also. Average pins from both sides (if customers' shoulders are even) and place pin at that amount from the seam. Chalk pins on wrong side of fabric. Remove pins.

2. Sew shoulder seams over chalk lines. If one end of original shoulder seam will be used, be sure to overlap stitching to have a secure seam. Be sure taper is straight.

3. Sew facings the same amount the shoulder seam was sewn at the same area. If dress is lined, sew lining the same amount as dress shoulder seam was sewn in that area.

4. Remove original shoulder seam where altered. Trim seams to original width.

5. Press seam open or as originally pressed.

6. Reattach facings and lining (if applicable) as original.

7. Press.

Sleeveless Dress Sides In

This alteration is most commonly done when the dress gaps out under the arm or hangs too low under the arm. If the dress is very large, it may need to be taken in more than one place. The easiest way to take it in is through the side seams. This narrows the armhole and will bring it up higher. Be sure that the armhole is not too high under arm. If so, it may irritate the underarm when worn. Check for princess seams or a center back seam that may also need to be taken in, if the dress is very large. To fit for side seams taken in: pinch loose fabric at bottom of armhole and pin. Continue down side of dress placing pins 2-3" apart. Place pins accurately, making the fit consistent all the way down. A horizontal pin can be placed at the location to stop taking in the seam or if needed, pin through hem.

1. Average pins from opposite seams, side seams, front princess seams or back princess seams. Place pins that amount and direction from seam.

2. Detach armhole facing and/or lining from sleeve at bottom of sleeve. Chalk pins on wrong side of fabric. Remove pins.

3. Stitch side seam over chalk lines. Backstitch at top, overlap with a smooth taper at horizontal pin. If side seams are taken in through the hem, backstitch at bottoms.

4. If the dress is lined, take the lining in the same amount as the dress. If not, take the armhole facing in, the same amount as the dress at top of the side.

5. Remove original stitching where taken in. Trim seams to original width. Serge cut seams.

6. Repress seams as original.

7. Reattach facings and lining as original. Turn right side out.

8. Lightly press from outside.

Skirt Waist/Sides In

If the waistband is one piece, it will need to be detached, shortened, and then reattached to the altered skirt. If the waistband has side seams, go through them. If there is a center back seam, or belt loops, you can go through the center back.

To fit: have the customer face the mirror, pinch fabric to be taken in at top of waistband along side seam, continue down the seam, pinch fabric to be taken in and place additional pins 3-4" apart having pins in the exact location the seam needs to be taken in. A horizontal pin marking where to stop can be placed in the seam. You may be able to go down a few inches, or you may need to go down the whole skirt and through the hem. *After fitting, garment fabric should lay flat at the seam pinned in when on, not pulling in any direction.*

1. Average the amount pinned in on the sides, place averaged pins evenly from each side seam (at same distance from the top of skirt). Chalk pins on wrong side of garment. If the garment is lined, you will need to go under that. Measure the amount to be taken in at the waist, record. Remove pins. The waistband will need to be detached just before the side seam, along the front if the opening is in the back (or along the back if the opening is in the front), through the side, and the end the button is attached. Mark with a chalk dot or safety pin where the button will be relocated (over the amount waistband is to be taken in). Detach button. Mark with a pin and then on wrong side with chalk where new end of waistband will be located (over the amount waistband is to be taken in). If the waistband extended past skirt opening with a seam in bottom of waistband, record extension amount or place a safety pin (over the amount waistband is to be taken in) at new location at bottom of waistband.

2. Stitch side seams over chalk lines. Backstitch at top and bottom or overlap stitching about an inch if the altering begins in the side seam. Be sure taper is smooth and will lay flat when pressed open. Trim side seams to original width or just a little wider. Serge seams. If the skirt is lined, take lining in the same amount as skirt. Trim and serge seam.

3. Press skirt seams open or as original. Press lining seam flat. Baste lining to skirt ¼" from raw edge across top of side seam where opened.

4. Finish button end of waistband as original to the shorter length. If the waistband extended past skirt opening with a seam in bottom of the

waistband, record extended amount or place a safety pin (moved over the amount the waistband is to be taken in) at new location at bottom of waistband.

5. Pin button end of waistband to skirt opening, extend as original amount (if applicable). Evenly distribute band to slacks and pin in place. *This can be a job that three hands work better than two. To get some help, what I would do sometimes, is to place the waistband under the presser foot, put the presser foot down, and then hold skirt/waistband away from machine, thus getting an even distribution. Place a pin in the center holding waistband and skirt together, place a pin in the center of that, continue until entire waistband is evenly pinned to the skirt.* With the same seam size as original, attach waistband as original, overlapping original stitching at just before where detached, stitch in fold of waistband with right side to right side of skirt. Stop at skirt opening, backstitch.

6. The back of the waistband will need to be attached. Usually the back is attached by stitching in the ditch of the waistband seam catching back of waistband. *This can be tricky to achieve. You may need to hand baste back in place first.* Pin waistband in place making sure all is flat before stitching. Be sure when machine stitching that waistband is feeding evenly into machine.

7. Press. Resew button at chalk dot or safety pin (should be directly at top of zipper).

Skirt Waist/Sides Letting Out

Skirts may or may not be able to be let out. Places to let out possibly are: side seams, center front or back seams, darts, or pleats. Possibly the zipper can be removed, and reattached with a smaller seam. There may or may not be enough fabric to even go to all that trouble. **Things to tell the customer: Seams let out may show, especially if the garment is not new. If letting out the waist, you may have to add a piece of fabric to the waistband and it may not match exactly. Show fabric examples if they are handy to get at. If the customer is concerned, suggest they go to the fabric store and find a suitable fabric for use.** Letting out darts or pleats to enlarge waist area would be my preferred location to let out. If the skirt needs to be let out below darts it will need to be let out in another area or both. Determine if the customer needs more let out in the sides, front area, or the back area (by their body type and the style of the skirt). That is the area to let out. To fit for letting out waist: measure skirt on the customer with waistband unfastened and zipper unzipped. Measure amount from the button to ¼ inside of the buttonhole on the side closest to the button. This gives a bit of ease when skirt is buttoned. That is the amount to let the waistband out. Place a pin that amount vertically from top of zipper or record amount. Go down to middle of zipper, measure amount from zipper side to zipper side. Place a pin that distance on one side of zipper or record amount. Place a horizontal pin at the location to stop letting skirt out or record location. If the skirt needs to be let out below bottom of zipper, check fit for tightness in proportion to skirt at zipper area. Gauge amount needed to be let out. Check to see how much fabric is available in side seams to let out when garment is off customer to see if it is doable.

1. Detach waistband from just before the area to be let out through button end of waistband.

2. Determine the amount to be let out and from where. For example, if 1" needs to be let out through the front of skirt, and there are 2 front darts, let each dart out ½" or resew the dart seam ¼" over (to be smaller) from the original (there is ¼" on each side of dart, hence a total of ½" per dart). Some darts are marked with a mark that could be visible if let out all the way. If it is visible you will need to at least leave a narrow seam with the mark in it. Some darts are marked with a small hole cut into fabric. You will need to at least leave a narrow seam with the hole in it. If the skirt is lined, and the lining has darts, let them out the same amount that was let out in skirt. Remove original dart or seam stitching. Press darts to center.

3. The waistband or facing will need to be extended the amount let out in the waist. Find a similar color and weight fabric for this. Measure the entire width of the waistband: front, the front seam, the back waistband fabric and seam or turn under. Add a little room for error if desired. This can always be trimmed later. The length of fabric should be the amount to be let out plus ½" (for a ¼" seam where attached and at end). Interface the fabric for waistband as original waistband is.

4. Open up end of waistband. With front edges even, stitch extension onto waistband in a ¼" seam. Backstitch both ends. Press seam open. Mark with chalk or a pin on the extension where button will go (the amount to be let out over from original placement). Mark with chalk or a pin on extension where end of waistband will be (the amount to be let out over from original end of waistband). Trim to exact width needed. Finish waistband back as original, with serging, turned under, hem tape, etc. With right sides of waistband together, fold along top edge at button end. Stitch end as original was done at marked location. Trim seam. Turn right side out. Waistband should lay flat and even. Press.

5. Pin end of waistband to garment center front or opening, extending as original amount. Evenly distribute band to skirt and pin in place. *This can be a job that three hands work better than two. To get some help, what I would do sometimes, is to place the waistband under the presser foot, put the presser foot down, then hold skirt/waistband away from machine, thus getting an even distribution. Place a pin in the center holding waistband and skirt together, place a pin in the center of that, continue until entire waistband is evenly pinned to the skirt.* With the same seam size as original, attach the waistband as original, overlapping original stitching at the start, stitch in fold of the waistband with right side to right side of garment. Stop at center front/button end, backstitch.

6. The back of the waistband will need to be attached. Usually the back is attached by stitching in the ditch of the waistband seam while catching the back of waistband. *This can be tricky to achieve. You may need to hand baste back in place first.* Pin waistband in place making sure all is flat before stitching. Be sure when machine stitching that the waistband is feeding evenly into machine and not bunching or being pushed or pulled by the presser foot.

7. Press. Resew button at chalk dot or safety pin (should be directly at top of zipper).

CHAPTER 6
SUITS, JACKETS AND COATS

You may have heard of the story how some of the military leaders were disconcerted by soldiers wiping their nose on the proud uniform of Napoleon. Thus, there were orders that the brass buttons should be sewn on the front of sleeves. There are sources that claim that the origin of sleeves buttons was in the 18th century. It has carried on to this very day. Not for the same reason thankfully.

SHORTEN SUIT JACKET SLEEVES

Altering jacket sleeves are not easy but they are very doable and when you understand the methods it is very rewarding to be able to do a good job. When altering, doing all or almost all stitching on the machine is the goal. It usually is stronger, more even, and better looking than hand stitching. Until you are comfortable with this alteration, I suggest you alter one sleeve at a time, if you get stuck, you can use the other one to refer to. Determine desired finished length of sleeve by averaging pins or using the most accurate one. When marking, I have found that the most accurate place to mark/pin the jacket sleeve is just above the thumb. If the customer has different length arms, you should measure with a ruler the desired length amount above the thumb knuckle, or where the thumb attaches to hand, anywhere you can measure each hand accurately.

Things to share with the customer: If jacket sleeves are to be shortened a lot, and if extra width of fabric in underside of vent does not extend up more than 1" above finish line, sleeves will need to be shortened with "no vent method".

If there are cut buttonholes under the buttons the button placement will have to remain as the original, after the sleeves are shortened. If uncut buttonholes are under buttons, the stitching can be removed and buttons moved.

To fit for desired length of sleeve: Have customer put jacket on and button front buttons. With neck centered and lapels even, have customer relax arms at their sides. Turn excess sleeve fabric under to inside at desired length. Pin around entire sleeve if the customer approves of folded under length. If arms are different lengths, pin up each sleeve. A good place to use as a guide is the thumb knuckle. There is a range of desired lengths. If the customer is not sure, pin up a couple different lengths for them to choose, perhaps each sleeve a different one. The front pin above the thumb would be your most accurate pin. Keep this in mid when determining the finish line.

1. With sleeve laying flat, place a pin on the bottom fold below each pinned spot on the pinned up sleeve. Remove pins holding up sleeve. Use the pin above the thumb or average the amount to be shortened from all pins. If averaging, leave only one pin in the sleeve marking that location. This is your finish line pin. *Usually sleeve linings in suit jackets have a topstitched area in the sleeve seam that is the "easy in, easy out seam." Remove this topstitching to have access to the inside sleeve. If the lining is attached at the armhole seam to the jacket you will have to open up both sleeve linings. If you can reach through the jacket to the other sleeve you can open up just one sleeve, and pull the other sleeve through this opening to work on it. If the lining is attached at the hem with blindstitching, that will be where you will go inside, remove the blindstitching.*

2. Remove all cuff buttons. Safety pin the lining to the jacket fabric 4-6" from the hem if they are not tacked together near there.

This will assure that the lining does not get twisted upon reattachment Some sleeves are tacked or stitched together here. If the sleeve seams are sewn together near the hem and you are unable to work easily, safety pin the sleeve seams together somewhat higher on the sleeves, then remove the tacking. Detach jacket sleeve from sleeve lining at hem. Remove interfacing if it is the sewn in type. *In jacket sleeves the old fold line is the straight line, not the old cut line.* If decorative buttonholes have been used, they may need to be removed if they are the wrong location for a button after the alteration is done. If they are in the same or close location to where the new placement of buttons will be, they can be left and the buttons can be sewn over them when alteration is done. You may need to remove the bottom one or two and leave any above that. Or you may need to remove all. *Some buttonholes are sewn with a chain stitch. If so, use extreme care when removing them so the fabric is not damaged. Try to remove stitching from the underside of fabric first. That is the side the chain would pull from and less damage to fabric probably would be done using this method.* If decorative buttonholes are left in, you may not have access to the hem being loose from under the buttonhole. If this is the case, after removing the buttonholes that would have been too low for the new sleeve length, cut the hem free from just below the last buttonhole. Open vent about 3" above finish line to have room to put back together.

3. Chalk a line 2" below the new finish line pin. Measure that amount from the old finish line and chalk that at 2-2½"" increments all the way around. These chalk marks are your cut line. Measure the amount cut off and cut that amount off of the lining. If jacket sleeves are both to be altered to the same length, measure the same amount below the old finish line on the other sleeve and cut outside fabric. Cut lining the same amount. If jacket

sleeves are to be altered to different lengths, do this same process to the other sleeve's finish line pin. Do not press out original finish lines. *Sleeves may have functional or decorative buttonholes under the buttons. These may need to be removed. If they are cut it is easiest to leave them and place the buttons over them after the sleeve length is altered. You may need to hand stitch the sleeve hem at an angle/miter under them. If they are decorative buttonholes, removing the stitching will allow you to place buttons at the original distance from the finished edge of the sleeve or at standard placement. Most customers do not care about this, but to be sure you are not removing a look they want, it is best to ask for permission to do this, since you will be changing the original application.*

Variation: hem is cut longer at sleeve vent to be under all buttons with no cut buttonholes. Open up entire hem through sleeve seam to alter length of sleeve. Mark length and cut off 2" below new finish line pin using old fold line as a straight line. If the seam needed to be opened above the vent to get hem out, restitch sleeve seam to top of vent. *If the buttonholes are cut, it is easiest to leave them and place the buttons over them after the sleeve length is altered. You may need to trim, fold, and hand stitch the sleeve hem at an angle/miter under them as you will not have room to machine stitch a seam.*

4. If original fused interfacing in sleeve is not as wide as the hem, cut more and fuse or sew in interfacing as original to finish line on wrong side of fabric. *If you have a 2" sleeve hem ideally you have a 2" strip of interfacing.*

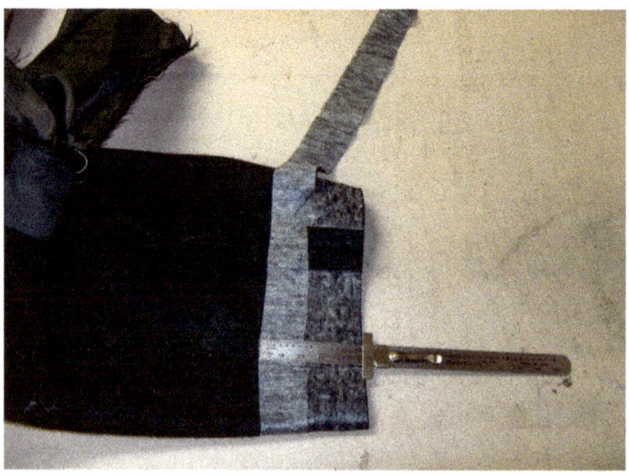

Match weight of original interfacing or close to it. A stiff interfacing in a thin fabric will show and will not look good. A light interfacing in a thick fabric will not do the job. If the original interfacing was a sew in type, sew back in as original.

If jacket sleeves are to be shortened to within 1" of the top of the vent you will still be able to leave a vent but it will take some time to get things laying correct, you may want to suggest closing the vent with a straight seam. If the top of the vent is at the desired finish line or below it, you will have to close the vent with a straight seam.

5. On wrong side of sleeve, place a pin 2" from the cut edge at the inner arm sleeve seam, and another on the back side at seam near button vent area 2" from cut edge. Place the vent pin in the front sleeve along the vent fold line and 2" up from cut edge.

To firmly hold hem in place: At inside seam fold seam together at pin and stitch seam close to original seam stitching, backstitching at the bottom edge, stop at ½" below cut end with backstitching. *This free ½" of seam will be needed when attaching jacket to lining.*

If the sleeve is tapered or gets narrower through the hem, you may need to have less fabric in the hem seam than in the sleeve seam, so it lays flat when done. The sleeve seam that runs down the inside of the arm is where the alteration should be done. Determine how much wider the sleeve hem needs to be to lay flat. At about 1" above the finish line pin, place the machine needle in the stitching. Stitch over original stitching to the finish line. Begin to taper out from that point, with a straight line to the end of the hem. The seam in hem at end of seam could be as little as ⅛". The sleeve seam above the finish line should still be ½". Remove original seam stitching below finish line in hem. Press hem seam open.

6. The hem needs to be firmly held in place at the sleeve's inside seam. It can be tacked together there by hand, stitching only ¾" below cut edge of hem or sewn on the machine. I prefer to do it by machine. To do so, fold the right sides of the seam together at the finish line. Turn the bottom of sleeve so that the seam is on the right side and the sleeve is on the left. In the seam, stitch both the sleeve seam and the hem seam, starting near the finish line, ending about ¾" below cut edge of hem. When turned right side out the hem should have a crisp line along the finish line.

MITERED SLEEVE: The front sleeve mitered cuff is commonly used in tailored jackets. It lays flatter than just straight seaming it, but is a little tricky to get the hang of. Do not press out original stitching line. *This will be used to get a parallel line so the miter is correct.* Measure the amount from the corner finish line pin (where the hemline and folded vent fabric meet) to the mitered seam. Chalk or use a lead pencil to mark a parallel line that amount over from miter seam (marked line should go through the finish line pin location). Fold at pin placing old mitered seam on top of itself. Backstitch and stitch along chalk or pencil line. Turn right side out.

The sleeve bottom should lay flat and even. Reach inside hem and push seam to be open in miter. Pin flat for pressing. Sleeve should be straight across with front sleeve the same length as the back sleeve at the vent. Steam and lightly press mitered seam open from top. Remove pin, steam and lightly press again. The finish line pin should be at the fold on the bottom of sleeve.

SLEEVE WITH A VENT BUT NO MITER: If sleeve is tapered or gets narrower through hem you may need to have less fabric in the hem seam then in the sleeve seam so it lays flat when done. The sleeve seam that runs down the inside of the arm is where the alteration should be done. Determine how much wider the sleeve hem needs to be to lay flat. At about 1" above the finish line pin, place the machine needle in the stitching. Stitch over original stitching to the finish line. Begin to taper out from that point, with a straight line to the end of the hem. The seam in hem at end of seam could be as little as ⅛". The sleeve seam above the finish line should still be ½". The hem needs to be firmly held in place at the sleeve's inside seam. It can be tacked together there by hand, stitching only ¾" below cut edge of hem or sewn on the machine. I prefer to do it by machine. To do so, fold the right sides of the seam together at the finish line. Turn the bottom of sleeve so that the seam is on the right side and the sleeve is on the left. In the seam, stitch both the sleeve seam and the hem seam, starting near the finish line, ending about ¾" below cut edge of hem. On front sleeve, fold hem up with right sides together at pin. With hem up and sleeve down, backstitch and stitch starting at finish line pin. Stop ½" from cut edge of hem. Fold back cut edge of hem to bottom, as pictured. Continue stitching to end of folded edge, backstitch.

Turn right side out.

Sleeve should be straight across with front sleeve the same length as the back sleeve at the vent. The finish line pin should be at the fold on the bottom of sleeve.

7. Resew bottom of jacket and lining sleeve seams if they have come out (where cut off). With right sides together place lining to be ½" longer than jacket hem at inner arm sleeve seam. With lining side down sew a ½" seam in jacket (1" seam in lining) to the vent keeping lining ½" longer than jacket in entire seam.

Overlap previous stitching, stitch from inner arm sleeve seam, in the other direction, to the vent, keeping lining ½" longer than jacket in entire seam.

8. Turn right side out through lining opening. Vent should lay flat. Bottom edge of vents should be even.

9. Press. *Use vinegar and water equal parts mixed in a spray bottle to remove old press lines in fabrics that will allow water on them.*

10. Topstitch lining entry seam shut.

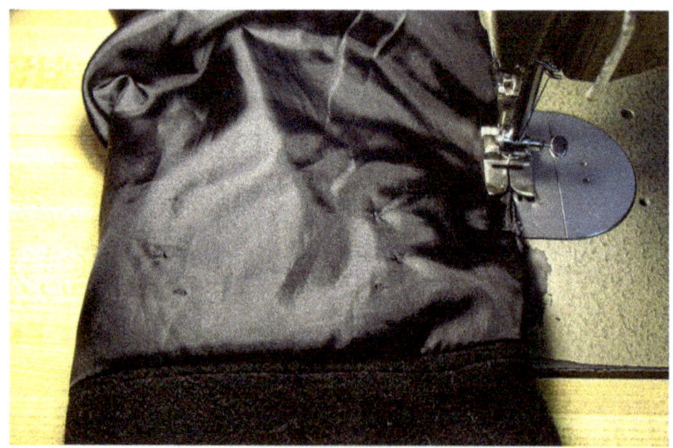

11. Mark for button placement on outside sleeve the same distance from seam as original placement (usually about ⅝" from seam). The first button from the bottom should be 1 ½" from edge.

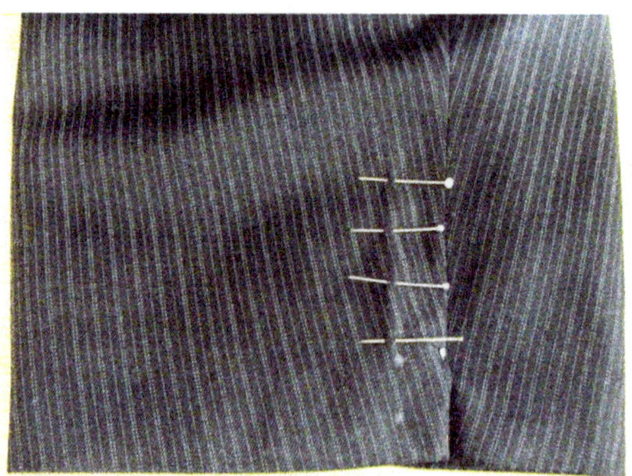

Most buttons used are ⅝". Buttons should touch but lay flat and parallel to the sleeve seam. Place a straight pin at 1 ¼" from bottom edge and ⅝" (or the original amount from the seam) over from the vent/seam. The second button from the bottom should be marked with a straight pin ⅝" (or the width of the button) above the first pin being parallel to the sleeve seam. The third button should be marked with a pin ⅝" (or the width of the button) above the second pin being parallel to the sleeve seam. The fourth button should be marked with a pin ⅝" (or the width of the button) above the third pin being parallel to the sleeve seam. Sew buttons on with the same color thread as the original. Some are stitched on with an X pattern, some are not. Duplicate original stitching. Hand stitching is safer, machine stitching is quicker but extreme care must be taken not to break a button with the needle. It can be challenging to see exact button placement if you are machine stitching the buttons on.

12. Press/steam along the hem line on the inside. Lightly press and steam from outside.

JacketSleeves Shortened with No Vent

Determine desired length of sleeve.

Open sleeve lining at inside elbow. If no topstitched area is on the lining seam of the sleeve, open a 4"-6" area at elbow area on inside of sleeve lining to enter and exit inside seams of the jacket. Safety pin sleeve lining to jacket in seam about 6" from hem to be sure when stitching back together you will line up sleeves with out twisting them. Open up the seam attaching lining to sleeve at hem. Open up tacking at seam or pull apart fusing (stitch witchery) holding hem up if that was used. Detach sleeve hem interfacing if sewn in type has been used. Press this flat for reuse. Cut off the amount to be shortened on outside layer of jacket and lining. The ideal hem for most jackets is 2". Not all manufacturers or styles of jackets use this. If it is a standard style and you would like to increase hem size to the 2" and enough fabric is available, try it. The amount cut off lining may need to be adjusted to reflect the amount of fabric added to the outside layer of jacket fabric. For example, if the original hem was 1 ½", you would be adding ½" to outside layer of jacket hem. If you are able to add ½" in the lining also, and you attach the lining to the sleeve at the old seam location, everything should line up fine. Another option is to leave an extra ½" in lining for possible lengthening later. If the previous seam had ½" of the lining in the seam, you could put 1" in the seam of the lining. Suit jackets are a clothing item that are more likely to be passed onto another person, or may be kept as the person grows, and may need to be realtered later.

Interfacing adds body to the hem and helps it lay nice. Fusible interfacing works well. Match weight of original interfacing if possible. If you cannot, error on the side of less weight versus too heavy of an interfacing. If a sewn in type of interfacing was used, fasten it along cut edge of jacket fabric with a ¼" seam using all and overlapping if extra. If original interfacing is short, you will need to use another piece to make it the entire edge of sleeve. Stitch lining to jacket starting at the inner arm seam with lining side down, jacket up.

If you are leaving 1" in the lining seam, be sure to align lining to be ½" wider than the jacket fabric in seam. Use care when stitching at seam area, seams are likely to open if pulled too hard where cut off and may need to be restitched so they do not open up above seam. Line up seams, lining may have more fabric then jacket, if so, ease in fullness throughout hem. Remove safety pins holding fabric together in middle of sleeve. Tack hem up in seams amount of hem. Most sleeves have two seams. Tack hem in place in both seams amount of hem. If the jacket has only one seam it maybe adequate. If not you may want to add stitch witchery to hold hem in place. Use caution with this method since the stiffness of the stitch witchery may show after it is fused especially on delicate to medium fabrics. You may want to hand stitch the hem in place with very small stitches so the thread does not show. The weight of the hem may show anyway. Some hems may be topstitched. I would recommend to duplicate whatever method the manufacturer has used. To help the hem and lining be more secure, stitch lining to jacket together about 4" in the long sleeve seams.

Turn right side out. If everything looks good, the lining sleeve can be closed. Press hem.

Shorten Jacket or Coat Sleeves with a Sewn on Cuff

To mark sleeves for finished length, pinch the amount to be shortened in sleeve and pin. Continue around entire sleeve, trying to pin in about the same amount.

1. If the coat is lined, open up the lining. *Most sleeve linings in suit jackets have a topstitched area in the sleeve seem that is the easy in, easy out seam. Remove this topstitchting to have access to the inside sleeve.* When looking at the sleeve, the amount from the pin to fold of pinched area would need to be doubled. On inside of sleeve chalk the pin on the top fabric and on the bottom fabric at each pin, remove pins, then average the amount between the chalk lines, that will be the amount to be shortened.

   If you are relatively new to this I would recommend doing one sleeve at a time, it allows you to refer to the other one if there are any questions. Safety pin lining to jacket in seam 4"-6" above cuff seam if there is a lining, so alignment of seams will be correct when reattaching. Remove cuff. Walk cuff up seam and repin with safety pin in seams near elbow area of sleeve. If cuff seam was not lined up with a sleeve seam measure amount on sleeve from the nearest seam, and record that amount. If there is no seam or if there are other markings, record that measurement with the cuff so when it is sewn back on it will be at the correct placement. Move cuff up to elbow area of sleeve (keeping right side to right side) and pin above where originally placed.

2. Cut off the amount to be shortened from lining and outside fabric of jacket (begin measuring from cut edge of sleeve). If the seams above cut edge have opened up restitch them. If sleeves are now wider than the original width of the bottom of the sleeve they will need to be tapered to the size of the original width. They can be tapered from elbow area down or from underarm seam if needed as long as the customer does not need the fullness in the upper arm. They can be tapered on one seam or more.

3. Starting at sleeve seam safety pinned together, sew cuff to jacket sleeve in the same depth seam as original. Cuff and sleeve bottom should be the same width.

4. Starting at the seam safety pinned together, with right sides together, sew lining to jacket sleeve over the stitching line just sewn. Safety pin can be removed holding lining to jacket after beginning to stitch the seam.

5. Turn jacket right side out. If there was top stitching on original application duplicate as original. Repeat with the other sleeve. Sew sleeve lining shut if entry to inside was gained there.

6. Press

Shorten Coat Sleeves with a Seam/Trim Above Finish Line

Mark finished length on one sleeve or both if sleeves are different lengths. Average the amount pinned. If the amount to be shortened is pinned up and customer likes the amount left below seam/trim you will be able to leave that and shorten from hem. Otherwise alter as follows: If the coat is lined, to gain access to the inside go through bottom of coat, if it is unattached. If it is attached at hem, open a lining sleeve seam in elbow area (check for a topstitched area). If the sleeve is tacked to lining in underarm seam or other places this may need to be removed. Safety pin the coat sleeve and lining sleeve together in the underarm sleeve seam before removing it to keep sleeves lined up correctly.

1. Open up sleeve at seam/trim. Cut off bottom of sleeve still attached to coat the amount to be shortened. Center lower sleeve on upper sleeve at seam.

2. Sew sleeve sections back as original. Detach lining from bottom of sleeve. Cut lining off the amount cut off of upper sleeve. Resew lining to bottom of sleeve. Place a pin at finish line in sleeve seam, fold up and tack sleeve/lining seam to sleeve seam in as many seams as there are to hold hem secure. Remove pins.

3. Press.

Lengthen Jacket or Coat Sleeves

Some jacket sleeves are finished at the bottom with a miter in the hem. If this is the case and if the mitered seam is trimmed, jacket sleeves will not be able to be lengthened.

To fit: Measure how much longer the customer would like the sleeve to be. I liked to hold a short ruler at the sleeve bottom and slowly lower it until the desired finished length was at the bottom of the ruler. And the amount to lengthen is right there on the ruler. At least ⅜" fabric should be left for hem. Record the amount to be lengthened on the invoice. Place a pin the amount to be lengthened parallel to the bottom edge. Place another pin forming at. This means to lengthen the pinned across amount.

1. Remove buttons at sleeve bottoms if there are any. Record the placement of them from the bottom, sleeve seam, and distance from the next button. Open sleeve lining seam 4-6" long at elbow for easy entering/exiting if lining is attached at garment hem. Safety pin lining seam to outside layer of coat in seam to keep sleeve alignment correct so when reattaching the lining, it does not get twisted. Detach sleeve lining from coat sleeve at hem. Detach any tacking or fusing holding the hem in place. Cut sleeve lining at center of sleeve parallel to bottom of sleeve on a straight line all the way around. *This is where extra lining fabric will be inserted. This method allows lining at bottom of sleeve to match coat lining exactly. Visually you will not see the inserted fabric from the outside but you may catch a glimpse of the lining at the sleeve bottom.*

2. Cut a strip of similar color and weight lining the amount sleeve is to be lengthened x 2 plus 1" wide. This allows for the length added in the lining, the outside layer of coat, and the seams where inserting. For example: If the sleeves need to be lengthened ¾", the strip of lining to be inserted in center of sleeve lining would need to be 2 ½" wide. The length of the strip needs to be the width of the sleeve lining where inserting, with a little extra for the seam. After cutting the sleeve lining for insertion, lining

sleeve seams will probably need to be restitched at cut edge so they will not open up.

3. Sew lining strip to sleeve lining right sides together at bottom edge of the cut with a ¼" seam backstitching at the beginning and end of seam (if piecing through the sleeve opening) or overlapping seam 1" (if going through sleeve lining with no opening). Sew lining strip to the other sleeve piece (same side of the coat/jacket) with right sides together. Lightly press insert seams, taking care not to crease coat sleeve. Repeat on the other sleeve lining. Serge seams.

For lengthening with ¾"or more left in hem: The seam attaching lining to the bottom of the sleeve can be ½" or less. If the original was ½" I would probably just leave it as it was.

For lengthening with ⅜"- ¾" left in hem. You can make the seam attaching lining to the bottom of sleeve as little as ⅛"-¼" depending on the durability and quality of the fabric The seam needs to be secure. Serging or zigzagging the seam will add strength.

4. Resew bottom of jacket and lining sleeve seams if they have come out.
    Match lining and coat seams up and pin in place. Stitch the lining to the coat at the hem with the amount of seam you have chosen. If there is an excessive width of lining, stitch the seam with the lining side down. The machine will naturally feed it through a little more on the bottom.

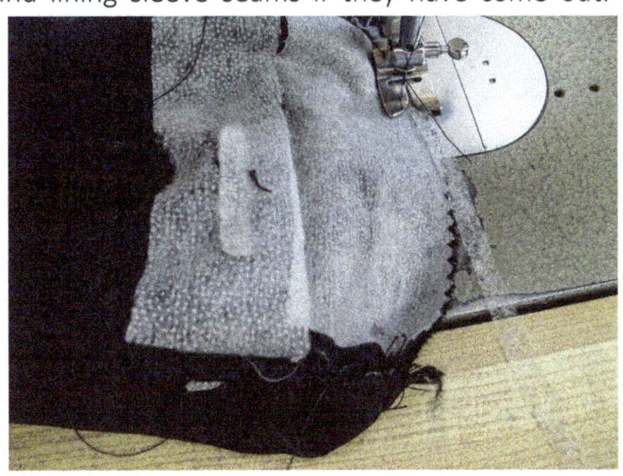

Using a fusible web (such as stitch witchery) cut a strip ¼" wide, place it on the wrong side of sleeve hem at the raw edge. Stitch with large stitches over seam line through webbing. *You may choose to hand stitch hem edge to secure in position instead of using the fusible web.* Tack hem up at seams. If a fusible web was not used, fold hem up amount needed and hand stitch in place keeping stitches invisible from the right side. With hem flat, place lining and sleeve seams even. Baste from a couple inches above hem for about 4"-5" or as can. Repeat for other sleeve seam. This is to keep sleeve hanging correctly when done.

Sleeve with No Vent

Resew bottom of jacket and lining sleeve seams if they have come out. Match lining and coat seams up, pin in place.

For lengthening with ¾" or more left in hem: Place a pin in coat seam at finish line. Fold seam at pin. Machine or hand tack seams together at the end of the hem. The small hem may need to be hand stitched (keeping stitches invisible from right side) along entire hem to hold in correct position.

4. Sew lining to coat at hem as original. With hem flat, place lining and sleeve seams even. Baste from a couple inches above hem for about 4-5" or as you can. Repeat for other sleeve seam. This is to keep sleeve hanging correctly when done.

For lengthening with ⅜"-¾" left in hem: Sew lining to coat at hem with a ¼" seam, overlap stitching 1" at end. Using a fusible web (such as stitch witchery) cut a strip ¼" wide, place it on wrong side of sleeve hem at the raw edge. Stitch with large stitches over seam line through webbing. *You may choose to hand stitch hem edge to secure in position instead of using the fusible web.*

4. Tack hem up at seams. If a fusible web was not used, fold hem up amount needed and hand stitch in place keeping stitches invisible from the right side. With hem flat, place lining and sleeve seams even. Baste from a couple inches above hem for about 4-5" or as you can. Repeat for other sleeve seam. This is to keep sleeve hanging correctly when done.

Sleeve with a Vent but No Miter

Place a pin at the inner sleeve seam at the finish line, and each side at seam near button vent area. Resew bottom of jacket and lining sleeve seams if they have come out.

For lengthening with ¾" or more left in hem: At inside seam, fold sleeve at finish line, pin and stitch in the seam close to original stitching up to ½" from cut edge, backstitch. This free ½" of seam will be needed when attaching jacket to lining. Or machine or hand tack seams together at the end of the hem.

On inner sleeve, fold at pin and stitch in the seam close to original stitching up to ½" from cut edge, backstitch. Or machine or hand tack seams together at the end of the hem.

If sleeve is tapered or gets narrower through hem you may need to have less fabric in the hem seam than in the sleeve seam so it lays flat when done. For example, if seams are ½" wide and sleeve tapers through hem, with right sides together, start by backstitching, stitch the back sleeve vent seam in a ½" seam (at the finish line pin), lay hem flat with a 2" hem along edge, continue stitching seam and stop ½" from cut edge. The seam in hem at end of seam could be as little as ⅛". The sleeve seam should still be ½".

On outer sleeve, fold with right sides together at pin. With hem up and sleeve down, backstitch and stitch starting at pin. Stop ½" from raw edge of hem. With wrong sides together, fold back raw edge of hem towards bottom of sleeve. Continue stitching to end of folded edge, backstitch. Remove pins.

4.   Match up sleeve seams and sew lining to coat at hem as original.

For lengthening with ⅜"-¾" left in hem: At inside seam, fold at pin, tack hem up.

On back sleeve, fold at pin, stitch seam to end, backstitching at both ends.

On front sleeve, fold at pin, stitch seam to end, backstitching at both ends. Remove all pins.

4. Match up sleeve seams and sew lining to coat with a ¼" seam. Using a fusible web (such as stitch witchery) cut a strip ¼" wide, place it on wrong side of coat at hem edge of fabric stitch with large stitches over seam line through webbing. You may choose to hand stitch hem edge to secure in position in stead of using the fusible web. If a fusible web was not used, pin hem up amount needed and hand stitch in place keeping stitches invisible from the right side. Baste sleeve seam to sleeve lining seam from a couple inches above hem for about 4-5" or as can. Repeat for other sleeve seam. This is to keep sleeve hanging correctly when done.

5. Turn right side out. At seams, measure hem amount from bottom edge to where the seam lining is attached, on inside of sleeve at hem first, press that same amount along entire bottom of sleeve, steaming and lightly pressing as needed to fuse hem to outside layer of coat. Use caution net to over press. Using a press cloth may be a good idea depending on your fabric. A fabric with a nap or texture may press better using a damp press cloth or towel. Sleeve should be straight across with front sleeve the same length as the back sleeve at the vent. The finish line pin should be at the fold on the bottom of sleeve. Topstitch sleeve lining shut at opening/openings. Remove finish line pin.

6. If buttons were on the sleeves sew back with original placement from the bottom edge and sleeve seam.

7. Steam/press as needed.

Jacket Sides In

Fitting: With the jacket on customer, and even on each side of the neck, have the customer button it up. When purchasing a jacket, shoulders should be the width of the widest part of his arms. So the sleeve hangs straight down from the shoulder. If there is an overhang off the shoulder the jacket may be too large and may not be worth the expense of doing a lot of alterations to the customer. *Narrowing the shoulders is a big job, the sleeves need to be removed, shoulder pads and all interfacings need to be narrowed, sleeve headers need to be removed and resewn in, the linings needs to be narrowed, etc. In most cases it would be a better investment to have the customer get a smaller suit.*

Have the customer lift their arms up such as would be done for driving or dancing. Ask him if he or she would be doing those activities, and how much room they would like for movement. The usual place to take a jacket in is in the seam just to the back of the sides. This seam is through the hem and goes to the back of the armhole. If the jacket is quite large it may need to be taken in through the center back seam also. Keep in mind that this will only take the back in, the front will be as original and if the back is taken in a large amount the front may hang funny. If they would like it taken in at the area the side seam joins the sleeve seam or higher, you will have to go into the center back seam. Begin pinning at the top of the jacket and go down. If the jacket is too big at the back by the collar, you may need to take the collar in with a seam in the center back of it. If so, let the customer know you will be putting a seam in where there was not an original seam. When pinning in side seams make sure the back vent lays flat and not open. To pin sides, pinch coat in with the seam in center of pinched fabric. Slant pins (taper) at top of seam under armhole so the jacket lays flat. Leave enough room to get into seam under armhole at top of side seam (about ½-1"). If the jacket needs to be taken in through the armhole, it is a lot of added work and a different fee. Pin center back seam in if necessary tapering at top and bottom above vent (if there is one) so jacket lays flat.

1. Open up about 5" in the center of the topstitched side of center back vent at hem. If there isn't one, open up the seam attaching lining to jacket about 6" to get to inside of jacket. If sides are to be taken in through hem, both sides at the hem will need to be opened in addition to the vent opening. If hem is tacked at seams, stitched down or fused, open it up near side seams.

2. Average pins on side seams. Chalk those pins on the wrong side of jacket. If center back seam needs to be taken in, chalk those pins on inside of jacket. Remove pins.

3. Stitch side seam over chalk marks starting about 1" below top chalked spot, stitch up to seam and overlap ½" or so, pivot jacket with needle down and stitch down jacket to end. Overlap bottom stitching or backstitch if through hem. Repeat for other side seam.

4. Take lining side seams in the same amount as jacket was taken in.

5. If the center back seam needs to be taken in, start stitching seam about 1" above top chalked spot, stitch in seam down jacket tapering to a smooth line above top of vent. Take center back lining seam in the same amount as jacket.

6. If jacket seam was pressed open, remove original stitching to just below where stitching has been overlapped at end of alteration area. I like to leave some extra fabric in the seam for possible letting out in the future, but the seam needs to lay flat when pressed. Maximum amount to have in the seam would be 1- 1½"fabric on each side of stitched seam. Trim if needed. Press seam flat. Press lining seam flat.

7. With right sides together at side seam in hem stitch seams together up to ½" from edge of hem to hold hem in place. Or you can tack in place after the lining is attached.

8. Turn jacket right side out. With one hand laying seam flat and open (remove hand before actually pressing), lightly press and steam side seam open.

9. Sew lining to jacket at hem as original.

10. Sew vent seam shut as original. Press as needed.

Jacket Sides Out

With unbuttoned jacket on customer, measure the amount from top button to ¼" inside the parallel buttonhole. Mark that amount parallel to button with a pin and record. Measure the buttons from the waist, bottom, or top of pocket to know where on the jacket each amount needs to be let out. Repeat on each button and buttonhole.. The usual place to let a jacket out is in the seam just to the back of the sides. This seam is through the hem and goes to the back of the armhole. The center back seam can also be let out but it probably has a cut on one seam at the top of the vent. So the top of the vent is a good place to stop letting out in the center back seam. *If as much fabric is needed as possible, the vent can be let out on one side, it requires a bunch of time, and use care to be sure vent hangs straight when done.* When fitting, check to see that the vent is closed in back. If it is, and laying flat, the bottom of jacket will not need to be let out, taper amount to be let out to bottom of jacket, leaving that as original. Check to see if there is enough room through the back of jacket above armholes. If more room is needed the center back seam can be let out some, there is not usually much fabric. Have the customer hold arms out in front of him to check for room needed. This is a separate alteration and another charge. Usually the side seams are let out up to as high as you can get the machine in sewing a straight seam but if as much as possible is needed, the sleeve can be opened at the top of the seam and let out. This requires a lot more work, is more expensive, and usually I would recommend a larger jacket, depending on the situation of course. To do that the sleeve also needs to be let out at the top, in the seam, and tapered to the original. The following instructions do not include that alteration.

1. Open about 5" in the center of the back vent topstitching to gain access to inside of jacket. Turn jacket inside out. Check to be sure there is enough fabric in seams to let out the desired amount. If the jacket needs to be let out a total of 1" at the waist, the two side seams will need to be let out ¼" at waist (¼" on the front and back of each side seam will total 1"). Detach jacket from lining at hem if the alteration will go through it.

2. Serge the edge of jacket seams and lining to be let out if not already done.

3. Overlap seam stitching about ½" above seam area to be let out and with a smooth taper, stitch seam over the amount to be let out at each marked spot tapering at bottom or through hem as needed. Repeat with other side.

4. Let lining out the same amount.

5. Remove original stitching in seams where let out.

6. Press lining flat. Press jacket seam flat. With jacket laying flat on ironing board, and side seam open with one side over jacket and one side on board, press jacket seam open.

7. Turn jacket right side out. With one hand laying seam flat and open (remove hand before actually pressing), lightly press and steam side seam open.

8. If sides were let out at hem, turn jacket inside out at side hem. Fold right sides of seam at hem along original fold line. Stitch seam together (on one side of seam) from finish line to ½" from cut edge. This is to hold hem in place. Reattach lining to jacket as original. Turn right side out. Lightly press.

9. Close vent with topstitching as original. Press as needed.

Relining a Coat

If the coat is a winter coat you may choose to use a flannel back satin lining (my first choice). Buy the best quality one offered at your fabric store. With as much work as it is you want it to stand up as long as possible. Otherwise I choose a 100% polyester lining. It comes in many colors. To determine the amount of fabric needed, measure a piece at the widest place. Then measure the longest place. Add the amount of the seam on each side of the piece. That is the amount of fabric needed for that piece. I like to use ½" seams. It is a little more secure seam and gives you a tiny bit of room for error. Measure the rest of the pieces the same way. You can lay a yard stick on the floor and another across at a 90 degree angle. Lay your pieces down going the same direction lengthwise on all pieces. Figure out how many pieces you could lay out across for 44/45" wide lining and for 60" wide lining. Determine the length of fabric needed for each. Now you are prepared no matter what width the fabric you choose is. You may want to use a little heavier duty thread when sewing this. Leather coats are usually used for a long time. You want the thread to hold up. Quilting thread may be a good option. Monitor your tension. Lining fabric requires less tension, leather more.

1. Some shoulder seams are treated differently. Be sure to look at construction when removing lining. Make notes and/or safety pin pieces as originally sewn for referral if desired. Detach existing lining. If outside buttons are sewn through the lining, make a small cut around the button to leave button stitching secure but to free lining. If you're unable to do this, detach and record location for resewing on after lining has been replaced. Separate back, front, side (if one is used), and one sleeve. *The easiest way is usually to use a straight edge razor blade. Use extreme caution not to damage coat.* If the sleeve has two pieces, separate them. If there are duplicate pieces that are the same for each side, use the one in better shape. Reline front pockets if needed. Most lining pockets have a front and back that may be different sizes. You may want to do one pocket at a time to have one to refer to. *These will be used as your pattern.* If the front lining has a breast pocket, remove that. This may be used again if it is in good shape. Or the pocket may be replaced and the welts reused if there are any. Coat will need to be put back as original. After detaching the lining pieces you may want to label them with chalk, or even with a pen. Remove brand and care labels, if sewn to lining.

2. Press back, one of two front piece or pieces, and one sleeve piece or pieces. Mark pocket placement on new same side front piece.

3. Lay lining pieces out on fabric with the straight grain going the same direction on all pieces and cut. Be sure to cut two pieces of duplicate pieces (front, front sleeve, back sleeve, etc.).

4. Sew manufacturer label back as original. Sew back to side (if one is used) and then to front at side seams and shoulders stitching care label in original location. If the shoulder seams are not the same length, you will need to sew part of the shoulder seam to the facing at shoulder seam. The shoulder seam should go back as the original.

5. Sew sleeve seams leaving one sleeve seam open about 6-8" at center of sleeve (at inside elbow area). This will be used to turn coat right side out when done unless coat lining is not attached to coat at hem. If that is the case, sew sleeve seam completely. Serge all seams. Sew sleeve into body of lining matching center top of sleeve to shoulder seam. Restitch sleeve seam ⅛" inside seam for strength.

6. Press lining.

You may want to switch thread to a heavy duty one and your needle to a leather needle when actually sewing on the leather. When stitching the lining to the leather or coat, the lining fabric may feed into the sewing machine unevenly. It is crucial to lay lining and coat flat, pin it in the seam line to the leather or coat and remove pins just before you get to them.

7. Construct and sew pockets back in coat as original. If a breast pocket with a welt was originally at inside lining, put back as original.

8. Begin at the top of center back of lining, with right sides together, attach lining to center back of coat at facing with the same width seam as original. Pin entire neck edge checking to be sure shoulder seams line up. Stitch neck edge as original. Pin both sides of lining to coat with correct placement of lining at hem. Stitch in place.

9. Attach lining to garment at lower edge as original, matching side seams. Tack hem to garment as original.

10. At bottom of armhole, line the lining and coat sleeve seams up and follow them to the bottom edge, place pin at lining seam to coat seam at hem. Pin around hem. Stitch sleeves to lining at hem as original. Tack and baste all areas as original, such as the neck area, and armhole area, bottom of sleeves, etc A strip of lining may have been sewn to the armhole of the lining seam and of the coat seam to hold it in place, if so, reattach as original. Turn right side out. Some garments are topstitched at the seam where the lining attaches except in the hem. Duplicate if desired. Sew sleeve lining shut by the topstitching seam.

Replacing Coat Pockets

Pockets can take a lot of use. I recommend using good quality fabric for replacing pockets. I recommend using 100% polyester lining for light weight lining fabric. For heavy weight lining fabric I recommend flannel back satin lining.

Getting the pocket placement can be tricky when stitching the pocket back in to get the bottom of the pocket facing down. You may want to mark the bottom of the pocket welt or coat with a safety pin to be sure you face pocket down since when coat is inside out you may have a hard time deciphering with what is up and what is down. To get to the inside of the coat in the pocket area you could: go through the bottom, between the lining hem and the outside fabric hem, if if it is not sewn together, you could open stitching in a sleeve lining inside arm seam and go in that way (if lining sleeves are not sewn to outside layer of coat), you could open up stitching in center of coat vent in center back bottom and go through there (if there is one), if none of those options are available, you will have to open up a seam in the sleeve lining or at hem where lining is attached to the outside coat fabric You may want to remove one pocket at a time and use the other one to refer to if needed.

1. Remove pocket lining fabric, only opening stitching necessary to remove lining. Pocket front and back may be different sizes depending on the application used. If both pockets in the coat are the same, (this is usually the

case) you may cut all 4 pieces from the first pocket removed. I allow at least ½" for the pocket seams.

2. If the front and back pieces are not the same size, determine which is the front, and which is the back (you may need to refer to the other pocket to determine this). Place one right side of pocket lining piece along coat pocket as original placement. The pocket should have at least ½" pocket lining fabric at top edge when lined up. Excess of fabric can go to bottom for pocket depth. Pocket lining should have ½" in seam, coat welt or coat fabric may have less. Stitch seam. Check to be sure everything is laying flat, if so, sew down seam again. Align and sew other pocket piece to coat welt or coat fabric as original with ½" clearance at top edge or so and having ½" in lining seam, and original amount in coat welt or coat fabric seam.

3. Usually there is a small triangle piece of fabric on coat at top and bottom of pocket opening between front and back pocket pieces.

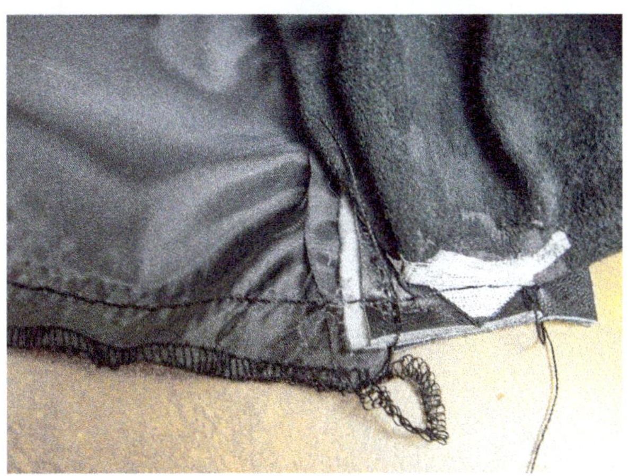

This needs to be stitched to pocket lining so there are no openings in the pocket. Refer to pocket not opened if needed. When stitching triangle down be sure pocket lining is laying flat from the previous seam stitched through triangle area. Stitch triangle to pocket lining. Check to be sure everything is good, if so, sew down seam again ⅛" from first stitching line in seam. Check pocket from outside to be sure all is laying flat. If so, turn back inside out, and sew pocket front and back together beginning at triangle. Seams in front and back pockets may or may not line up from side to side. Laying flat is more important that lining up even. Seam must be at least ½" wide at all places. Seam may be zigzagged in seam or serged if fabric is fraying. If the seam is a little more than ½" wide, extra fabric may be left in and not trimmed. Original pocket may be fastened to coat with a strip of fabric or tape to keep it in position, if so, reattach to new pocket as original.

CHAPTER 7
ZIPPERS

REPLACING A COAT ZIPPER

A sewn in coat zipper should not gather or wave when in coat, it should lay flat. Lining and outside fabric should be a little loose with zipper flat.

1. Remove old zipper keeping it attached at very top and very bottom. This is for referral when attaching the new one at this area. Some applications have an outside flap covering the zipper,

some have a flap to the inside,

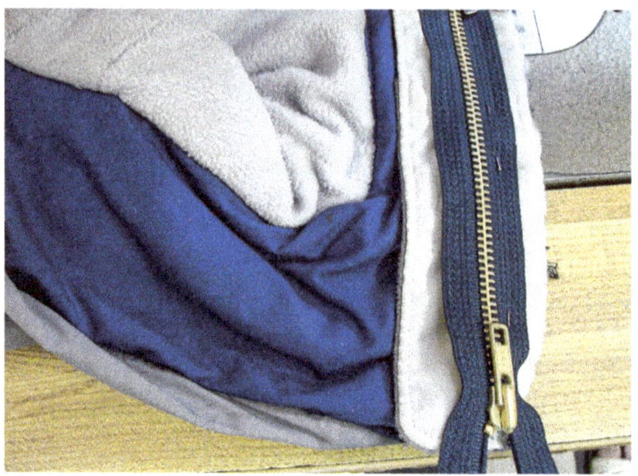

some have narrow flaps on each side, etc. *Using a razor blade can enhance the speed of removing a zipper. Caution should be used not to damage the coat or to get cut. Using a sharp razor will aid in not having to put a lot of pressure on it to cut threads.* Remove all visible loose threads.

2. Stitch over previous stitching lines attaching back facing or top facing that covers zipper to coat as original, if applicable. If a narrow flap was originally used on each side of zipper, stitch each to the zipper as was originally placed to zipper.

3. Pin zipper in place at bottom right side lining, placing the zipper's bottom edge at the same location as the original. Place the pin in the center of the zipper tape over the old seam line just above the stiff bottom of zipper. Line up the right side of coat (lining, zipper, and outside coat fabric) with the zipper pinned in place. Zipper should be taunt, coat and lining should have just a little ease.

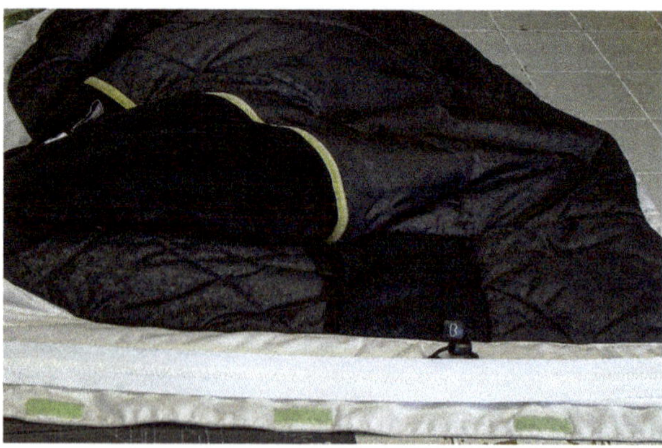

Pin zipper to top edge of lining with this placement. Pin a few more places on lining evenly distributing zipper and lining. With the wrong side of lining down on sewing machine and zipper (slide side up) placed over it, center zipper tape over the old stitching line on lining, stitch length of zipper beginning at the bottom. Lining should feed into machine nicely and not be gathered.

4. Shorten zipper if necessary.

Shortening a zipper: Trim zipper tape with pinking shears to about ¾" above desired length. Remove teeth to ⅛" below desired length.

Useful tools: end nippers to remove zipper teeth, and stops, and needle nose pliers (shorter nose is stronger). The strongest place on the needle nose pliers is at the center of the joint.

Place top stop in position, and open needle nose pliers so the center of the joint is over the top stop just above the top tooth. Crimp zipper stop above and just touching top tooth. Check to make sure stop is on tight. Do not crimp the zipper teeth. Zip up zipper and push on stop to check if stop is secure enough. Stop should not move at all. Repeat for other side.

5. Zip up the zipper. Pin remaining lining to zipper at the top and bottom making sure it is even with sewn in side lining. If there are any seams in the lining, place a pin in the unsewn zipper side straight across from the finished side at the seam.

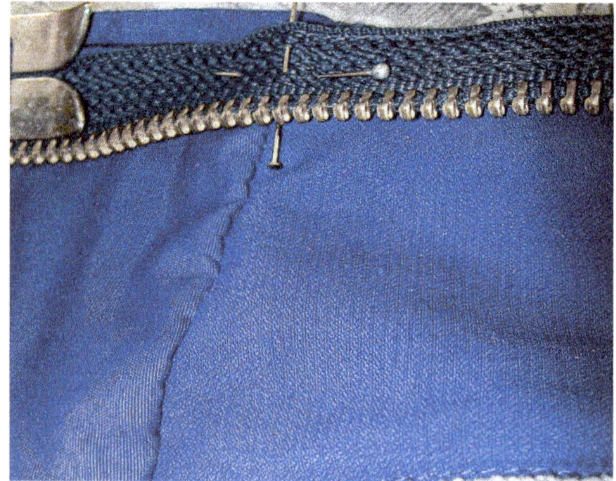

Pin the lining to the zipper every 4-5" or as needed with the seams lining up over the straight across pins.

6. With the wrong side of unsewn lining side down and the center of zipper tape placed over it, stitch length of zipper beginning at the bottom. Lining should feed into machine nicely and not be gathered.

7. Zip up zipper making sure that all seams and top and bottom are even. Unzip.

If the seam above top of the zipper was opened, restitch it as original. If the zipper was in it, duplicate as original. Pin outside layer to zipper/lining as original, evenly distributing fabric. Stitch, backstitching on both ends.

8. Mark any seams or designs on outside of coat with a pin straight across from finished side on zipper tape. Pin top and bottom outside layer to zipper/lining layer with seams over straight across pins. Leave straight across pins in until you stitch to them in case you need to check placement of outside fabric.

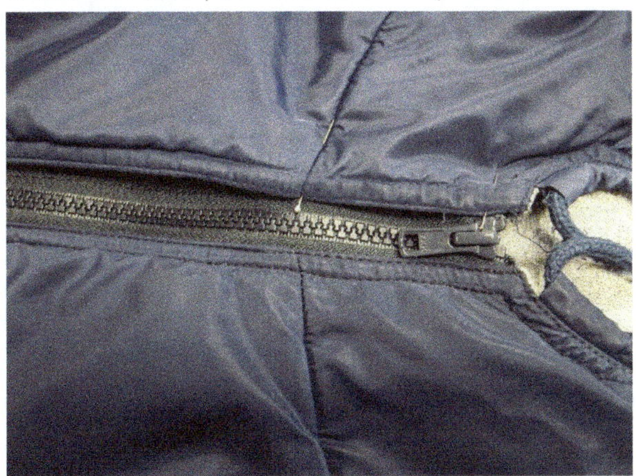

Stitch, backstitching both ends. Stitch another row if originally there were 2 rows of stitching.

9. A lot of coat zippers will have a bar tack at each bottom over the hard zipper tape area. It is a secure way to finish the bottom.

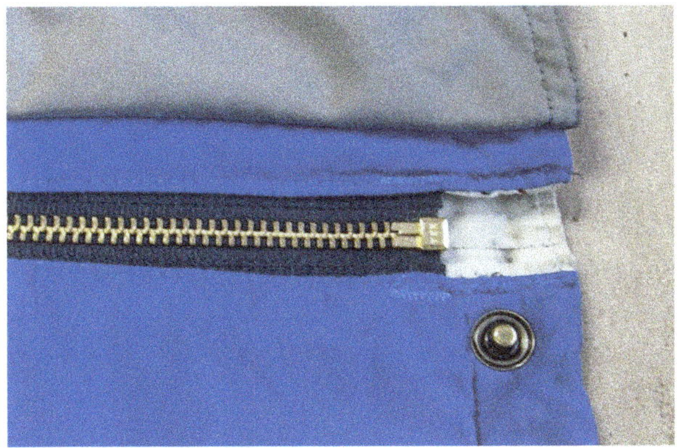

Duplicate as original. Resew any seam or hem top stitching that was removed for zipper removal.

10. Lightly steam and press using caution around plastic zipper parts.

Replacing a Leather Coat Zipper

Heavy weight leather is difficult to work on, it is heavy in weight, it is thick; it is hard for the needle to get through, and the original stitch lines cannot be duplicated exactly. They can be matched pretty well with a lot of care. I have actually gotten blisters before from working the hand wheel while working on the heavy leather. I had to eventually give it up, it was too hard on my hands to work the machine through it. You will probably need a heavy duty or professional machine to work on these.

Dress leathers are lighter, easier to get the needle through, but still the original stitch lines cannot be duplicated exactly. They can be matched pretty well with a lot of care. Not matching all original stitch lines is a big deal for some customers. Be sure to talk to them about this before replacing the zipper. I also used a Teflon foot that would glide easily over the leather. If you want to make good stitches I recommend using this. I liked to move the inside facing over (away from the edge of the teeth) if originally it was folded on the inside at the teeth. This would leave the old stitch holes in the facing at least at the top and bottom (I could move the facing over while stitching it to the zipper so I was stitching on the fold as soon as I could taper it smoothly). It would function better though and have less chance to get caught in the teeth when zipping up. Keep in mind that this is a more expensive item so you may be liable for error if something goes wrong. Follow the basic instructions for coat zipper replacement.

REPLACE JEANS ZIPPER

Directions are given for jeans with a flap over zipper on the jeans left side, if the flap over zipper is on the right side just reverse right and left when using these instructions. If you have a presser foot that will let you stitch ¼" away from the zipper teeth you may be able to use that. My machine had a useful setting that I could move the needle bar over to the right or left as desired so I was able to not switch feet out on a lot of applications. A zipper foot attachment will guarantee you are able to stitch where needed.

We used #5 heavy duty zippers for jeans.

1. Remove old zipper. *Sometimes the zipper is attached to the facing with a chain stitch. I suggest removing the topstitching first, check for possible chain stitching before detaching zipper. Chain stitching will rip cleaner and lots faster.* Remove all loose threads.

2. On jeans right side, place zipper with bottom stop where original one was placed, it should be just above where the bottom curved stitching or bar tack was on original application. Facing should be underneath zipper and jeans right side should be over the zipper about ¼" from zipper teeth. Pin facing, zipper, and jeans right side at bottom, line zipper up along the edge to top of denim, ease a little excess denim fabric in top layer, pin zipper to denim and facing at top edge also.

If zipper is too long: If zipper was originally inserted into waistband, trim top of zipper to be ½" longer than will be visible. Insert top of zipper into waistband. If zipper was not inserted into the waistband, the zipper may need to be shortened by removing zipper teeth and placing a stop on top. Finish zipper as it was originally done.

3. Stitch zipper to jeans beginning at bottom opening just to side of the bottom stop of the zipper, backstitch at top edge keeping waistband free. Stitch again if two rows were originally sewn.

4. Stitch along bottom edge of right side waistband with zipper and back facing in place, use caution not to hit a zipper tooth with the needle.

5. Zip the zipper, place a pin at top of unsewn side of zipper parallel to just under the waistband of finished side. This will need to be just under the waistband on left side when lining up for stitching. Unzip zipper.

6. On left side of jeans, open facing of zipper placket at bottom and line zipper up to original placement of stitch lines, usually you can see where the zipper teeth were originally.

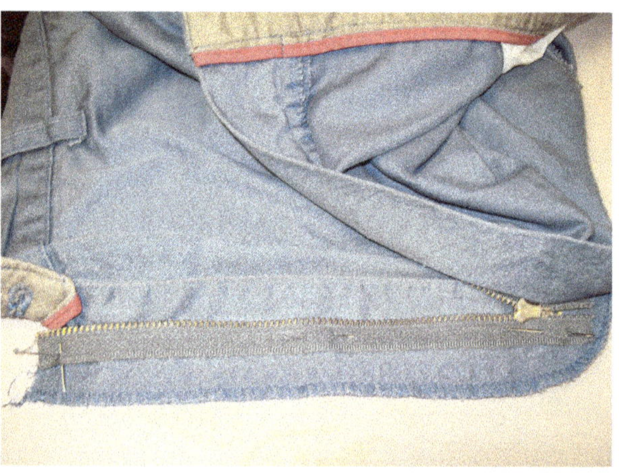

Zipper must lay flat at bottom across from where right finished side is attached. Pin zipper in place to facing. Zip up and check to see all is laying correctly from the outside. If so, unzip and stitch along side of zipper through facing. Check to see all is laying correctly from the outside. If so, stitch another line of stitching ¼" from first line of stitching through zipper and facing.

7. Turn facing back inside and tuck top edge inside waistband. Stitch along waistband through all thicknesses while holding or pin zipper and facing in correct position, use caution not to hit a zipper tooth with the needle.

8. Keep right side back facing out of the way, begin just below where the old bar tack was (or at the bottom of the straight stitching) on placket side and with the zipper zipped and laying flat, on the outside stitch along old stitch line starting at the bottom stitching up to waistband. You can either backstitch or just under the waistband take a stitch or two to where second row of original stitching is and stitch back down to just below where original bar tack was. Everything needs to be laying flat or you may need to remove stitching and do over. Check as you go to avoid unnecessary ripping.

9. Starting at the center front crotch seam about 1" below the end of stitches, stitch through all thickness up to bottom of curve of placket. Turn at just below zipper stop, following original stitching lines or close to them. Turn at old bar tack (should be overlapping other straight stitching on left side) stitch a couple stitches over and go down on second row overlapping existing stitching about 1" in crotch seam. Place bar tacks or straight stitch a couple times where original bar tacks where.

10. Press.

REPLACING A PANT ZIPPER

Most pants have similar construction techniques as the jean zippers. Use original type/weight of zipper or as customer desires. We used a lot of trouser #4.5 zippers. They are just a little heavier than standard pant metal zippers. Use instructions for jean zipper replacement with regular weight thread and topstitching as original.

REPLACING A COAT LINER ZIPPER

Remove zipper mostly leaving it attached about ½" at ends. Remove threads from coat. Place new zipper (with zipper slide up) on coat facing with bottom zipper separator placed just as original one was. Pin in place. Place a pin or mark where zipper stopped on other end. Remove old zipper completely from coat facing. Stitch zipper to coat facing with zipper side up and coat facing down to where original zipper stopped, backstitch. Shorten zipper if needed. Zip zipper. Mark unsewn zipper side at center of neck area and any seams with a pin. Pin center back mark of unsewn zipper (with zipper slide up) at center back right side of lining.

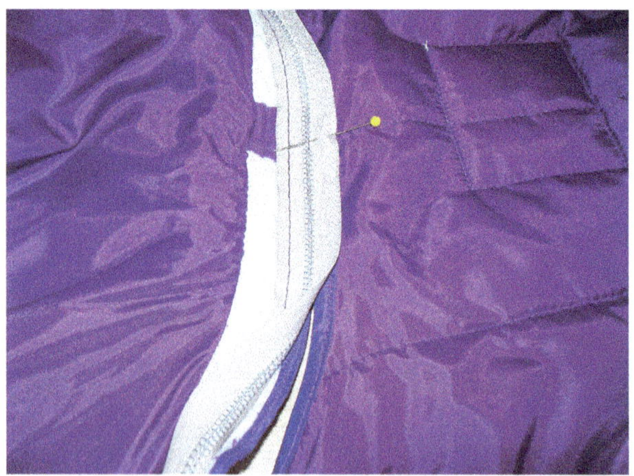

Pin the rest of lining to the zipper. Shoulder seams should meet and zipper should start and stop very close to original. Unzip. Stitch, backstitch. Can also be bar tacked on ends.

Replace Zipper
in Unlined Fleece Jacket or Sweatshirt

Remove zipper. Remove loose threads.

1. With zipper slide facing jacket pin the zipper at ¼" from bottom edge or at original placement. Zipper should be taunt and jacket should be loose. Pin at top edge. If zipper needs to be shortened it can be done now to length of original zipper, or after the fist side is sewn in. Evenly distribute fabric and pin to zipper a few more places.

2. Stitch with center of zipper tape placed over previous stitching.

    Zip up zipper. Shorten zipper if necessary. On unsewn side of zipper mark all seams, pockets, etc with a straight across pin. Unzip. Leave straight across pins in until you stitch to them in case you need to check placement of outside fabric.

3. Pin unsewn side of zipper to the other side of jacket placing pins at the respective seam, pocket, etc Stitch, backstitching both ends.

4. Zip zipper. Seams, pockets, etc should be across from each other. The bottom of jacket and top should be across from each other. Finish top edge as original above zipper.

5. Top stitch as original.

6. Bar tack at bottom of zipper both sides. Restitch any topstitching that was opened up to remove zipper.

7. Press.

Replacing an Invisible Zipper

Remove zipper. If the top of the seam that the zipper is placed in needs to be reinforced, do so. To correctly install an invisible zipper you must have an invisible zipper foot for your sewing machine. If you do not have one, make the investment, it is the only way to get a professional job. I have used plastic ones that can do the job. A metal one works more precisely.

1. Place top of the opened zipper with stop just below the top folded edge of the garment or just below the top of seam opening or just below the waistband (whatever application was originally used). The zipper will need to be turned out just enough to get the zipper foot in position. Once it is in place it should stay. I like to position the needle in the fold near the coil and lower the zipper foot into place. Do not stitch over the coil, this can damage it. Backstitch to end of zipper tape, (use caution when near the top stop, this can hang the foot up and may require some hand wheeling the machine along). *If there are any seams you will need to sew through, I have found that if you give a little room, or to stitch over just a bit from the coil (in the zipper tape), the zipper slide can function much better. You have a small amount of play in the foot, use it to your advantage. Let the machine feed the fabric, do not pull or push the fabric.* Stitch down to bottom edge of zipper. Stop at top of seam, backstitch. Check to make sure zipper closes/opens easily.

2. If there are any seams, designs, pockets, print etc that need to be matched you will need to mark on the unsewn zipper tape where it needs to line up on the fabric. To do this, zip zipper shut. From outside of garment, place a pin across (about ¼" from zipper coil) from exact location needed to match. Do this for everything that needs to be matched. Chalk pins on both sides of the unsewn zipper tape.

3. The bottom edges need to line up parallel. With garment wrong side facing you, and zipper zipped and laying over seam at bottom, place a pin through the zipper tape and seam. With zipper and seam laying flat, about an inch above pin or so, place the needle in zipper fold near coil and over old seam line. Stitch up to top edge of zipper, lining up all chalk marks on zipper tape to matching item. This can be a real trick. If you have a hard time doing this, you can start at the seam to be matched and baste some, start at the seam to be matched and baste some etc. The top of the zipper should line up at the top of garment across from the other side. Beginning about 1" above where stitching began, stitch going to top of seam, backstitch.

Zipper should lay flat, outside fabric should lay flat when zipped. All seams should be even, across from each other.

4. Restitch facing or waistband to top edge of garment as original. If garment is lined, reattach lining as original.

5. Sew hook and eye at top of zipper, if applicable. Hook and eye should hold garment shut above or at top of zipper. Place them just to inside of coil of zipper when stitching them on. Try to grab more than one layer of fabric (if possible) when stitching them on. See hook and eye instructions.

CHAPTER 8
OTHER

MILITARY UNIFORMS

Military uniforms may require patches to be sewn on, or alterations. Some of the patches now are attached with Velcro. I would recommend that you get a copy of or ask the customer or local recruiter what the specifications are for placement, how they are to be sewn, etc. Specifications for lengths and fit are also included in these. The different branches of the services will be different.

Fitting Tips: To measure the center of the upper arm for rank patch placement, measure from the very top of shoulder to the bottom of the bent elbow. Divide by 2 and place a horizontal safety pin there. If you are replacing a patch and the lining lays correctly (without any bunching or pulling) safety pin the lining to the jacket sleeve on all 4 sides before detaching original patch. Now your lining will be in the correct position when stitching. If this is a new patch, lining must be safety pinned in its correct location before stitching down the patch. Lining must be pinned (use safety pins) with a bit of excess on each side of the patch before new patches are sewn on. Each patch will take a little lining in the stitches also. If enough ease is not allowed in the lining the sleeve will not hang correctly and some bunching up of the outside fabric may occur. When attaching patch, mark the center of the patch and place over the safety pin. Mark the outside edges of the patch with chalk, or pins. Sleeve patches should usually line up on the outside of the sleeve. This can be quite tricky since the sleeve is not cut straight. To achieve a straight placement of patches when the jacket is on you must establish where the center of the sleeve is. To establish the center at the top of the sleeve can be done by marking the top of the sleeve at the shoulder seam or the center of the epaulet if there is one. As you go down the sleeve, the seam just to the back of the sleeve will hang pretty straight. At the bottom half of the sleeve you can use the center of the outside sleeve piece (measure the center between the two sleeve seams).

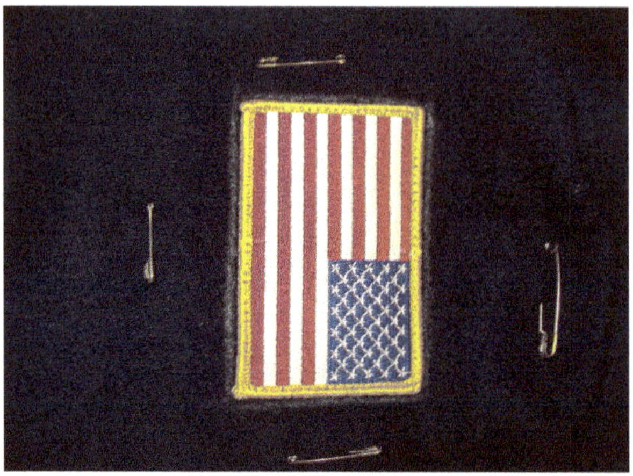

ATTACHING A LETTER TO A JACKET

Letters are usually stitched on jackets through the lining. Be sure the customer is okay with this. It can be very challenging to stitch only through outside layer of the jacket but it can be done. If this is desired see instructions at the end.

To attach a letter to jacket, center and line up to be straight and center per customer's wishes for position. Establish the center of the letter from top to bottom and from side to side. Mark with pins or chalk. Establish a straight line from center front edge and bottom of embroidered name or what ever straight line will be close to where letter will be attached. A straight line across can always be established by measuring up from the bottom edge of jacket. Pin a line under embroidered name or the near straight line the desired distance letter is to be placed from it. Pin another line the desired distance from the center front edge or other near straight line. Move the letter into position against both of these lines. Keeping that in place, place additional pins on the edges of the letter on each side and edge to have many visual placement aids. Pinning the letter onto the jacket distorts position and may not be accurate. Using a pin line will allow you to stitch the letter at the exact desired placement. Safety pin around the letter the lining to the outside layer of the jacket with the lining laying in the exact correct position.

Begin zigzagging if satin stitch was used, or straight stitch if serging stitch was used on letter with a medium width zigzag set on a short to medium stitch length. Stitch edge of letter pivoting at corners to just overlap when beginning next side. If the letter has an inside opening it may need to be attached to make letter stable. Continue stitching to where you started. Stitch over zigzagging for about an inch. Threads can be pulled to inside to secure permanently. Knot top and bobbin thread together. Trim threads with about a ⅜" tail.

To attach the letter only through outside layer of jacket, an opening will need to be made through the lining. Usually it would be in the sleeve inside elbow area, big enough to be able to keep lining free from under the jacket when stitching letter on. This requires some practice but can be done. After the letter is stitched on, the lining needs to be closed with a topstitching seam.

ELBOW PATCHES

Elbow patches can be made out of ultra-suede, ultra-suede like fabric, leather, or most durable fabrics. Ultrasuede can be washed and dry cleaned easily. Leather is not washable but can be dry-cleaned with special care. Any other fabric used will need to have the edges finished. A short stitch on the serger may work, or a satin stitch zigzag. Consider interfacing the fabric if it is not stiff enough. Try cutting patch large, mark desired size, and let the serger cut it as you serge. Or zigzag and then trim patch. If you are placing a patch on a worn sleeve, center it on the area most worn (should be the elbow). Otherwise you can have the customer try it on and mark with a safety pin where the elbow hits on the sleeve. There should be a sleeve seam in the patch area or near it. Use that seam for a straight line when placing the patch on the sleeve.

1. Center patch on worn elbow area. *To find center of patch, fold patch in half, fold in half again. The patch center is at the center folded spot.* Pin patch on through outside fabric only. Chalk along the entire edge of the patch. If the jacket is lined, you will need to gain access to the inside of the jacket. Most sleeve linings in the suit jackets have a topstitched area in the sleeve seam near the elbow area, that is the "easy in, easy out seam". Remove this topstitching to have access to the inside sleeve. If no topstitched area is in the sleeve seam, you will need to open the sleeve lining on the front sleeve seam about 8" or so near the elbow area to allow you to get inside of the sleeve with the machine. Put sleeve on machine with patch under presser foot and no other fabric under it but the pinned outside fabric. This may take some practice to be comfortable working in this small space but it will make for a professional job when done. The lining opening must be under the presser foot the whole time, so no lining will be getting stitched.

2. With a short stitch, stitch an even line near the edge of the patch, keeping the lining free from under the presser foot, at all times. Patch should be laying next to the chalk line. Continue around entire patch. Overlap stitching about an inch.

3. Close sleeve lining by stitching lining opening together in a narrow seam.

4. Press/steam patch.

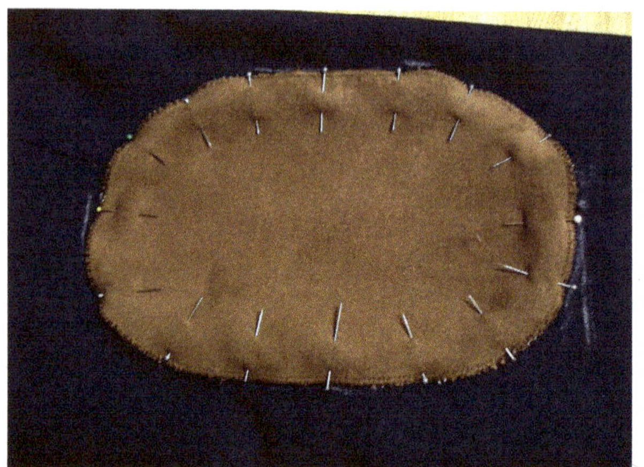

Jean and Other Garment Patches from the Inside

Measure area to be patched. If the fabric is weak near patch area, the patch may need to be enlarged to get to some secure fabric

1. Cut a patch the needed amount from similar colored and the same weight fabric

2. Serge edges of cut patch.

3. Center patch under area needed. To get it right the first time, place a safety pin in the center of the patch, center it from the outside in the center of the hole. Pin (from the outside of the garment) around edges using at least four pins, more as needed.

4. Using a regular weight thread that matches fabric color closely, stitch near the entire outside edge of patch from outside of garment. Usually you can feel the end of the patch from the outside with your finger. Stitch again ⅛" or ¼" from first stitching. Zigzag or straight stitch around hole. If there is a lot of weak fabric it is good to reinforce it by stitching through it and the patch many times. Straight stitching with the grain with small stitches is a good way to make less noticeable stitches. Outside fabric and patch should both lay flat.

5. Press.

Jean and Other Garment Patches from the Outside

Measure the area to be patched. If fabric is weak near patch area the patch may need to be enlarged to get to some secure fabric.

1. Cut a patch from similar colored (unless a contrasting patch is desired) and the same weight fabric the amount of patch needed plus 1" more for width and 1" more for length.

2. Press under ½" on all sides of patch.

3. Center patch over area needed. To get it right the first time, place a safety pin in the center of the patch, center it from the outside in the center of the hole. Pin from the top around edges using at least four pins, more as needed.

4. If the area to be patched is on a pant leg, unzip pants completely and place the area to be patched on the machine bed with no fabric underneath. Stitch around outside of patch stitching over the beginning spot about an inch. Stitch again ⅛"- ¼" from first stitching.

5. Press

Leather Hole or Tear Repair

Often we would get in a leather item with a tear in it. What I would recommend for the repair was to use a strong (such as silamide) but not a thick bulky thread that I would use to make small, even stitches to pull the leather together as original. Use caution with older leather as it my not be real strong. The stitches show but if evenly stitched, look "okay". This is a more permanent fix than to glue a piece of fabric or leather underneath the tear. On rare occasions I did do that though.

For a hole in leather the best thing to do would be to find a matching piece of leather and place it under the hole and stitch in place. Use centering technique explained in patching from the inside.

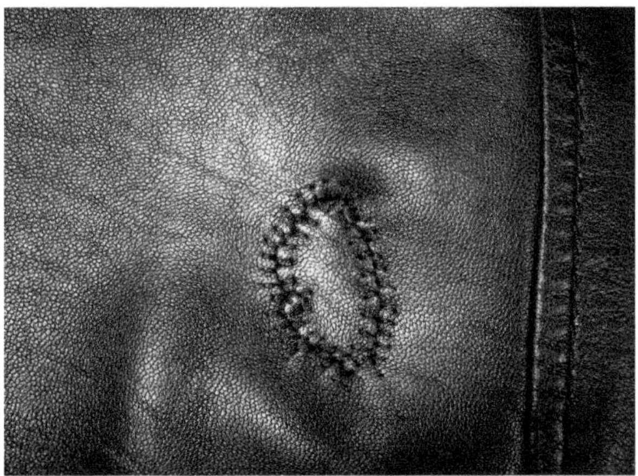

BRA CUPS

Sewn in bra cups are used on clothing that may not be able to have a bra underneath or the bra straps may be likely to show. To place in the correct position the garment must be on the customer. Hand each bra cup to the customer to place in position in front/under her breast. Pin each bra cup in place to garment from the outside. To protect the customer I slide a finger or two (to feel pin and push it back through) under the "in position" cup and pin with the other hand on the outside. Usually 2 pins hold it secure. The garment must have at least two layers or a seam going through the area bra cups will be stitched to, so you have fabric to stitch the cup to that will not show on the outside. Bra cup placement can be averaged or if customers breasts are uneven, bra cups can be stitched in just as pinned. Bra cups can be stitched on inside of dress lining or in between layers. To average bra cup placement; measure each cup from top of garment, center front, waist seam or yoke if available. Average each location measurement and place a pin there. Center bra cups among the pins. See picture. Pin cups in place beginning with center. Hand stitch cups in place with a large stitch catching only lining, not outside layer of fabric.

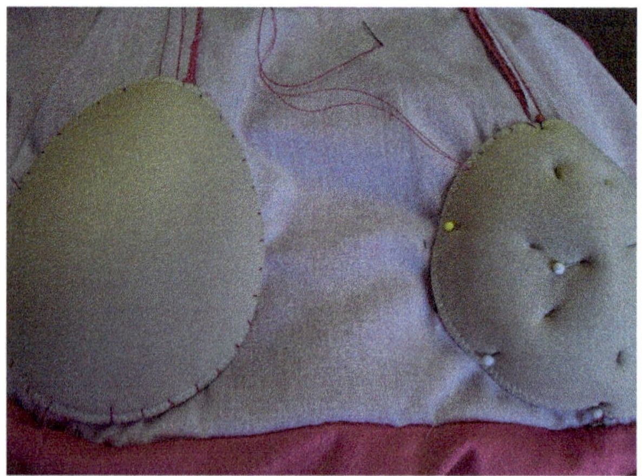

HOOK AND EYE'S

A hook and eye above a zipper is a good secure finish. Line hook and eye up to be just short of the center of the zipper so when it is hooked it will hold fabric together above top of zipper. To keep securely in position, stitch through seam or zipper tape below fabric. After stitching hook down through circular ends at least 4 stitches attach underside of hook to fabric by sewing a couple of stitches. This will hold it securely laying down. Knot thread next to fabric. Using needle go under fabric ¼" or so and then come up cutting thread there so thread end will pull below fabric. To keep eye in place, stitch loops each at least 4 stitches and then just above the loop, stitch across each side, to keep eye laying flat. Knot thread next to fabric. Using needle, go under fabric ¼" or so and then come up cutting thread there so thread end will pull below fabric

Buttons

Shirt buttons

Shirt buttons are usually sewn with regular weight thread. If there are 4 holes in the button it may be stitched straight across or in an X pattern. Generally using two strands of thread per stitch, 6 stitches per holes is a good amount. If more were used in the original application, use more. Thread color and stitch type need to be as the original to blend in. If the stitches are pulled tight holding the button right next to the fabric it may pull when buttoned. Some ease in the stitches will lay better when buttoned. If you will be machine stitching buttons on, you may want to use a heavy pin to hold the presserfoot away from the button, to give you some ease. Go slow and be careful, one wrong stitch could break a needle or the button.

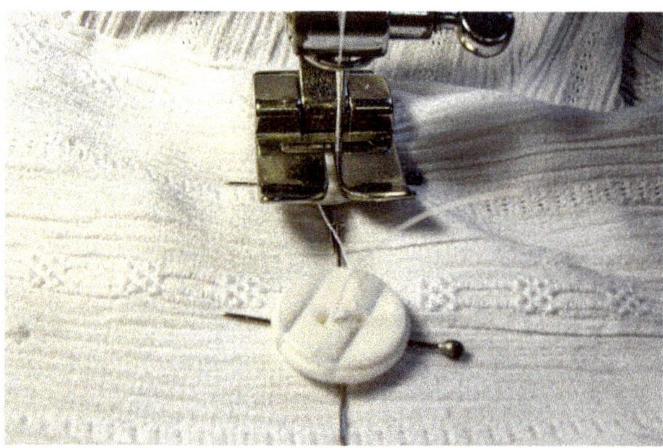

Pant Waist Button

Pant buttons are usually sewn with a shank. Regular or heavy duty thread may be used. Match original thread weight and color as the original if possible. Using a ⅛" - ¼" shank when button is sewn on allows the waistband to lay flat. Ideally the shank should be the width of the fabric the button will button through. To do that, allow enough thread when stitching so button is away from the fabric ⅛" - ¼". Generally using two strands of thread at a time, 6-8 stitches per holes is a good amount. If more were used in the original application, use more. Wrap thread around button thread/shank 4-10 times. Insert needle next to shank, and through the waistband. Knot next to fabric. Using needle, go under fabric ⅛" - ¼" or so and then come up cutting thread there so thread end will pull below fabric.

Coat Button

Buttons can be sewn on with waxed thread. It will help the button stand up and button easier. A shank longer than ¼" may need to be used, make it the width of the fabric to be buttoned through. Match original thread weight and color if possible. If backer buttons are used they are sewn on at the same time. Knot your thread and from the outside of garment insert needle at the center of where button is to be placed going through to the underside of fabric. Thread backer button onto needle and place it next to underside of garment. Insert needle in another hole in backer button and through garment to end up near the center of button placement location and through one hole of button. Holding button away from garment a little more than the desired shank amount, thread needle through another hole of button going through fabric and backer button. Go through backer button, fabric, and the first hole of button again holding button away from garment a little more than the desired shank amount the entire time. Do this at least 6 times. If the outside button has more than 2 holes repeat this process for the other 2 holes ending up on the outside with needle coming out below the button. Wind thread around shank tightly 6-10 times. Insert needle through fabric to back at button. Make a tight knot next to fabric. Using needle, go under fabric ⅛"- ¼" or so and then come up, cut thread there so thread end will pull below fabric.

Suspender buttons:

1. Back buttons should be placed 1 ¼" from center back seam in center of waistband facing.

2. Front buttons should be placed 1 ¾" from center side front (measure center between the side seam and center front of pants at zipper).

3. Sew with heavy duty thread using 2 strands knotted together to sew with 4 strands at a time. Stitch through each hole 3-4 times leaving a ⅛"- ¼" shank and wind thread around that 2-3 times. Put needle under waistband facing near button and come up ¼" away and knot, then go under facing again for ⅓" or so and come up and cut thread near facing so thread is not seen. Tug on facing so end of threads go under.

GLOSSARY

Application: method used to construct item

Alter: change

Bar tack: a narrow zigzag stitch with a satin stitch length

Blindstitcher: sewing machine that stitches (used on the underside) in an almost invisible chain stitch

Bottom Zipper Stop: the U shaped metal piece with sharp ends that bend over the zipper coil or teeth to stop slide

Chain stitch: a stitch that usually can be pulled out easily by grasping at the correct place

Connectors: Multiple threads/ ribbon/trim used to hold 2 pieces of fabric together, usually at the hem connecting lining and outside garment

Distributed: not all in one area

Finish line: the desired finished line on length of a garment

Flatlock Stitch: multiple thread stitch with 2-3 parallel rows and a zigzag type in the center all at the same time on the outside of fabric, the underneath a chain stitch

Hand Wheel: The wheel on the right side of the sewing machine that moves along with the needle bar. To "hand wheel" stitch: move the needle bar up and down by moving the hand wheel and not the foot control.

Inseam: seam on the inside leg of pants

Outseam: seam on the outside leg of pants

Overpressing: Pressing an item until it begins to get damaged

Pounding Block: A wooden block placed on steamed fabric to set a crease

Prepping: preparing item for repair or alteration

Right side of fabric: the side of fabric that is on the outside of garment

Rotary Cutter: tool with round blade used to cut

Satin Stitch: a short zigzag stitch that looks like satin when done

Seam Guide: a guide for fabric to align with to assure even stitching, can be adhesive or can screw into sewing machine bed

Stitch in the ditch: sewing over the previous seam on the right side usually to hold the underneath fabric in place

Tapered: going in or out, could be a straight line but not straight to garment

T-pin: a strong pin shaped like a capital T

Top Zipper stop: the C shaped metal piece that crimps above the zipper teeth to stop the slide from coming off the end of the zipper

Vent: an opening in a garment that is not closed, and lays one side over another

Wedge: a flat hard shaped piece of plastic used under the presser foot to keep it level and the stitches more even when sewing over bulky seams

Wrong side of fabric: the side of fabric that is on the inside of garment

Zipper slide: the metal piece that slides up and down either closing or opening the zipper

Zipper Tab: the handle on the slide

Zipper tape: fabric on the zipper

Seams Easy

3343 Southgate Court SW, Cedar Rapids, Iowa, 52404, 319-362-9339

Pants shortened or lengthened $16.00
Pants lengthened with tape $17.00
Lined Pants shortened or lengthened $21.00
Cuffed Pants shortened or lengthened $18.00
Lined Cuffed Pants shortened $23.00
Jeans shortened reattaching original hem $17.50
Trouser waist and seat in or out $18.00
Trouser thigh in $18.00
Jeans waist in or out $20.00
Pants or Skirt zipper replaced $19.00
Invisible zippers replaced .... $1.00 extra
Winter Coat zipper replaced $35.00
Carhartt zipper replaced .... $25.00 & up
Columbia Coat zipper replaced $52.00
Sweatshirt zipper replaced $23.00
Soft Leather Coat zipper replaced .... $45.00 & up
Top Coat shortened $45.00
Rain Coat shortened .... $30.00 & up
Lined Rain Coat sleeves shortened with straps & liner .... $29.00 & up
Dress or Skirt shortened .... $18.00 & up
Lined Dress or Skirt shortened .... $24.00 & up
Pleated Dress or Skirt shortened .... $26.00 & up
Replace waistband elastic .... $13.00 & up
Lined Jacket sleeves shortened or lengthened .... $27.00 & up
Lined Jacket sides in or out .... $27.00 & up
Lined Jacket center back seam in through collar .... $23.00 & up
Jacket collar lowered .... $28.00 & up
T-shirt shortened $15.00
Shirt tapered, flat felled seam .... $20.00 & up
Uniform Pants side stripe sewn on .... $20.00 & up
Uniform patches sewn on each.. $4.00
Uniform Jacket sleeves stripes sewn on $12.00
Leather Garment patches sewn on .... $6.00 & up

30% Extra Charge for less than 48 hours turnaround
Prices are subject to change without notice. November 2010